How to Get on in the World

in the World

A Ladder to Practical Success

Major A.R. Calhoon

Contents

HOW TO GET ON
IN THE WORLD
A LADDER TO PRACTICAL SUCCESS

BY

Major A.R. Calhoon

CHAPTER I
WHAT IS SUCCESS?

I t has been said that "Nothing Succeeds Like Success." What is Success? If we consult the dictionaries, they will give us the etymology of this much used word, and in general terms the meaning will be "the accomplishment of a purpose." But as the objects in nearly every life differ, so success cannot mean the same thing to all men.

The artist's idea of success is very different from that of the business man, and the scientist differs from both, as does the statesman from all three. We read of successful gamblers, burglars or freebooters, but no true success was ever won or ever can be won that sets at defiance the laws of God and man.

To win, so that we ourselves and the world shall be the better for our having lived, we must begin the struggle, with a high purpose, keeping ever before our minds the characters and methods of the noble men who have succeeded along the same lines.

The young man beginning the battle of life should never lose sight of the fact that the age of fierce competition is upon us, and that this competition must, in the nature of things, become more and more intense. Success grows less and less dependent on luck and chance. Preparation for the chosen field of effort, an industry that increasing, a hope that never flags, a patience that never grows weary, a courage that never wavers, all these, and a trust in God, are the prime requisites of the man who would win in this age of specialists and untiring activity.

The purpose of this work is not to stimulate genius, for genius is law unto itself, and finds its compensation in its own original productions. Genius has benefited the world, without doubt, but too often its life compensation has been a crust and a garret. After death, in not a few cases, the burial was through charity of friends, and this can hardly be called an adequate compensation, for the memorial tablet or monument that commemorates a life of privation, if not of absolute wretchedness.

It is, perhaps, as well for the world that genius is phenomenal; it is certainly well for the world that success is not dependent on it, and that every young man, and young woman too, blessed with good health and a mind capable of education, and principles that are true and abiding, can win the highest positions in public and private life, and dying leave behind a heritage for their children, and an example for all who would prosper along the same lines. And all this with the blessed assurance of hearing at last the Master's words: "Well done, good and faithful servant!"

"Whatever your hand finds to do, do with all your might." There is a manly ring in this fine injunction, that stirs like a bugle blast. "But what can my hands find to do? How can I win? Who will tell me the work for which I am best fitted? Where is the kindly guide who will point out to me the life path that will lead to success?" So far as is possible it will be the purpose of this book to reply fully to these all important questions, and by illustration and example to show how others in the face of obstacles that would seem appalling to the weak and timid, carefully and prayerfully prepared themselves for what has been aptly called "the battle of life," and then in the language of General Jackson, "pitched in to win."

A copy line, in the old writing books, reads, "Many men of many minds." It is this diversity of mind, taste and inclination that opens up to us so many fields of effort, and keeps any one calling or profession from being crowded by able men. Of the incompetents and failures, who crowd every field of effort, we shall have but little to say, for to "Win Success" is our watchword.

What a great number of paths the observant young man sees before him! Which shall he pursue to find it ending in victory? Victory when the curtain falls on this brief life, and a greater victory when the death-valley is crossed and the life eternal begins?

The learned professions have widened in their scope and number within the past thirty years. To divinity, law, and medicine, we can now add literature, journalism, engineering and all the sciences. Even art, as generally understood, is now spoken of as a profession, and there are professors to teach its many branches in all the great universities. Any one of these professions, if carefully mastered and diligently pursued, promises fame, and, if not fortune, certainly a competency, for the calling that does not furnish a competency for a man and his family, can hardly be called a success, no matter the degree of fame it brings.

"Since Adam delved and Eve span," agriculture has been the principal occupation of civilized man. With the advance of chemistry, particularly that branch known as agricultural chemistry, farming has become more of a science, and its successful pursuit demands not only unceasing industry, but a high degree of trained intelligence. Of late years farming has rather fallen into disrepute with ambitious young men, who long for the excitement and greater opportunities afforded by our cities; but success and happiness have been achieved in farming, and the opportunities for both will increase with proper training and a correct appreciation of a farmer's life.

"Business" is a very comprehensive word, and may properly embrace every life-calling; but in its narrow acceptance it is applied to trade, commerce and manufactures. It is in these three lines of business that men have shown the greatest energy and enterprise, and in which they have accomplished the greatest material success. As a consequence, eager spirits enter these fields, encouraged by the examples of men who from small beginnings, and in the face of obstacles that would have daunted less resolute men, became merchant princes and the peers of earth's greatest.

In the selection of your calling do not stand hesitating and doubting too long. Enter somewhere, no matter how hard or uncongenial the work, do it with all your might, and the effort will strengthen you and qualify you to find work that is more in accord with your talents.

Bear in mind that the first condition of success in every calling, is earnest devotion to its requirements and duties. This may seem so obvious a remark that it is hardly worth making. And yet, with all its obviousness the thing itself is often forgotten by the young. They are frequently loath to admit the extent and urgency of business claims; and they try to combine with these claims, devotion to some favorite, and even it may be conflicting, pursuit. Such a policy invariably fails. We cannot travel every path. Success must be won along one line. You must make your business the one life purpose to which every other, save religion, must be subordinate.

"Eternal vigilance," it has been said, "is the price of liberty." With equal truth it may be said, "Unceasing effort is the price of success." If we do not work with our might, others will; and they will outstrip us in the race, and pluck the prize from our grasp. "The race is not always to the swift, nor the battle to the strong," in the race of business or in the battle of professional life, but usually the swiftest wins the prize, and the strongest gains in the strife.

CHAPTER II
THE IMPORTANCE OF CHARACTER.

That "Heaven helps those who help themselves," is a maxim as true as it is ancient. The great and indispensable help to success is character.

Character is crystallized habit, the result of training and conviction. Every character is influenced by heredity, environment and education; but these apart, if every man were not to a great extent the architect of his own character, he would be a fatalist, an irresponsible creature of circumstances, which, even the skeptic must confess he is not. So long as a man has the power to change one habit, good or bad, for another, so long he is responsible for his own character, and this responsibility continues with life and reason.

A man may be a graduate of the greatest university, and even a great genius, and yet be a most despicable character. Neither Peter Cooper, George Peabody nor Andrew Carnegie had the advantage of a college education, yet character made them the world's benefactors and more honored than princes.

"You insist," wrote Perthes to a friend, "on respect for learned men. I say, Amen! But at the same time, don't forget that largeness of mind, depth of thought, appreciation of the lofty, experience of the world, delicacy of manner, tact and energy in action, love of truth, honesty, and amiability--that all these may be wanting in a man who may yet be very learned."

When someone in Sir Walter Scott's hearing made a remark as to the value of literary talents and accomplishments, as if they were above all things to be esteemed and honored, he observed, "God help us! What a poor world this would be if that were the true doctrine! I have read books enough, and observed and conversed with enough of eminent and splendidly-cultured minds, too, in my time; but I assure you, I have heard higher sentiments from the lips of the poor uneducated men and women, when exerting the spirit of severe, yet gentle heroism under difficulties and afflictions, or speaking their simple thoughts as to circumstances in the lot of friends and neighbors, than I ever yet met with out of the Bible."

In the affairs of life or of business, it is not intellect that tells so much as character--not brains so much as heart--not genius so much as self-control, patience, and discipline, regulated by judgment. Hence there is no better provision for the uses of either private or public life, than a fair share of ordinary good sense guided by rectitude. Good sense, disciplined by experience and inspired by goodness, issued in practical wisdom. Indeed, goodness in a measure implies wisdom--the highest wisdom--the union of the worldly with the spiritual. "The correspondences of wisdom and goodness," says Sir Henry Taylor, "are manifold; and that they will accompany each other is to be inferred, not only because men's wisdom makes them good, but because their goodness makes them wise."

The best sort of character, however, can not be formed without effort. There needs the exercise of constant self-watchfulness, self-discipline, and self-control. There may be much faltering, stumbling, and temporary defeat; difficulties and temptations manifold to be battled with and overcome; but if the spirit be strong and the heart be upright, no one need despair of ultimate success. The very effort to advance--to arrive at a higher standard of character than we have reached--is inspiring and invigorating; and even though we may fall short of it, we can not fail to be improved by every honest effort made in an upward direction.

"Instead of saying that man is the creature of circumstance, it would be nearer the mark to say that man is the architect of circumstance. It is character which builds an existence out of circumstance. Our strength is measured by our plastic power. From the same materials one man builds palaces, another hovels; one warehouses, another villas. Bricks and mortar are mortar and bricks, until the architect can make them something else. Thus it is that in the same family, in the same circumstances, one man rears a stately edifice, while his brother, vacillating and incompetent, lives forever amid ruins; the block of granite which was an obstacle on the pathway of the weak, becomes a stepping-stone on the pathway of the strong."

When the elements of character are brought into action by determinate will, and influenced by high purpose, man enters upon and courageously perseveres in the path of duty, at whatever cost of worldly interest, he may be said to approach the summit of his being. He then exhibits character in its most intrepid form, and embodies the highest idea of manliness. The acts of such a man become repeated in the life and action of others. His very words live and become actions. Thus every word of Luther's rang through Germany like a trumpet. As Richter said of him, "His words were half-battles." And thus Luther's life became transfused into the life of his country, and still lives in the character of modern Germany.

Speaking of the courageous character of John Knox, Carlyle says, with characteristic force: "Honor to all the brave and true; everlasting honor to John Knox, one of the truest of the true! That, in the moment while he and his cause, amid civil broils, in convulsion and confusion, were still but struggling for life, he sent the schoolmaster forth to all comers, and said, 'Let the people be taught;' this is but one, and, indeed, an inevitable and comparatively inconsiderable item in his great message to men. This message, in its true compass, was, 'Let men know that they are men; created by God, responsible to God; whose work in any meanest moment of time what will last through eternity.'

. . . This great message Knox did deliver, with a man's voice and strength, and found a people to believe him. Of such an achievement, were it to be made once only, the results are immense. Thought, in such a country, may change its form, but cannot go out; the country has attained *majority*; thought, and a certain spiritual manhood, ready for all work that man can do, endures there. The Scotch national, character originated in many circumstances; first of all, in the Saxon stuff there was to work on; but next, and beyond all else except that, in the Presbyterian Gospel of John Knox."

Washington left behind him, as one of the greatest treasures of his country, the example of a stainless life--of a great, honest, pure, and noble character--a model for his nation to form themselves by in all time to come. And in the case of Washington, as in so many other great leaders of men, his greatness did not so much consist in his intellect, his skill and his genius, as in his honor, his integrity, his truthfulness, his high and controlling sense of duty--in a word, in his genuine nobility of character.

Men such as these are the true life-blood of the country to which they belong. They elevate and uphold it, fortify and ennoble it, and shed a glory over it by the example of life and character which they have bequeathed. "The names and memories of great men," says an able writer, "are the dowry of a nation. Widowhood, overthrow, desertion, even slavery cannot take away from her this sacred inheritance . . . Whenever national life begins to quicken . . . the dead heroes rise in the memories of men, and appear to the living to stand by in solemn spectatorship and approval. No country can be lost which feels herself overlooked by such glorious witnesses. They are the salt of the earth, in death as well as in life. What they did once, their descendants have still and always a right to do after them; and their example lives in their country, a continual stimulant and encouragement for him who has the soul to adopt it."

It would be well for every young man, eager for success and anxious to form a character that will achieve it, to commit to memory the advice of Bishop Middleton:

Persevere against discouragements. Keep your temper. Employ leisure in study, and always have some work in hand. Be punctual and methodical in business, and never procrastinate. Never be in a hurry. Preserve self-possession, and do not be talked out of a conviction. Rise early, and be an economist of time. Maintain dignity without the appearance of pride; manner is something with everybody, and everything with some. Be guarded in discourse, attentive, and slow to speak. Never acquiesce in immoral or pernicious opinions.

Be not forward to assign reasons to those who have no right to ask. Think nothing in conduct unimportant or indifferent. Rather set than follow examples. Practice strict temperance; and in all your transactions remember the final account.

CHAPTER III
HOME INFLUENCES.

A careful preparation is half the battle." Everything depends on a good start and the right road. To retrace one's steps is to lose not only time but confidence. "Be sure you are right then go ahead" was the motto of the famous frontiersman, Davy Crockett, and it is one that every young man can adopt with safety.

Bear in mind there is often a great distinction between character and reputation. Reputation is what the world believes us for the time; character is what we truly are. Reputation and character may be in harmony, but they frequently are as opposite as light and darkness. Many a scoundrel has had a reputation for nobility, and men of the noblest characters have had reputations that relegated them to the ranks of the depraved, in their day and generation.

It is most desirable to have a good reputation. The good opinion of our associates and acquaintances is not to be despised, but every man should see to it that the reputation is deserved, otherwise his life is false, and sooner or later he will stand discovered before the world.

Sudden success makes reputation, as it is said to make friends; but very often adversity is the best test of character as it is of friendship.

It is the principle for which the soldier fights that makes him a hero, not necessarily his success. It is the motive that ennobles all effort. Selfishness may prosper, but it cannot win the enduring success that is based on the character with a noble purpose behind it. This purpose is one of the guards in times of trouble and the reason for rejoicing in the day of triumph.

"Why should I toil and slave," many a young man has asked, "when I have only myself to live for?" God help the man who has neither mother, sister nor wife to struggle for and who does not feel that toil and the building up of character bring their own reward.

The home feeling should be encouraged for it is one of the greatest incentives to effort. If the young man have not parents or brothers and sisters to keep, or if he find himself limited in his leisure hours to the room of a boarding house, then if he can at all afford it, he should marry a help-meet and found a home of his own. "I was very poor at the time," said a great New York publisher, "but regarding it simply from a business standpoint, the best move I ever made in my life was to get married. Instead of increasing my expense's as I feared, I took a most valuable partner into the business, and she not only made a home for me, but she surrendered to me her well-earned share of the profits."

A wise marriage is most assuredly an influence that helps. Every young man who loves his mother, if living, or reveres her memory if dead, must recall with feelings of holy emotion, his own home. Blest, indeed is he, over whom the influence of a good home continues.

Home is the first and most important school of character. It is there that every civilized being receives his best moral training, or his worst; for it is there that he imbibes those principles that endure through manhood and cease only with life.

It is a common saying that "Manners make the man;" and there is a second, that "Mind makes the man;" but truer than either is a third, that "Home makes the man." For the home-training not only includes manners and mind, but character. It is mainly in the home that the heart is opened, the habits are formed, the intellect is awakened, and character moulded for good or for evil.

From that source, be it pure or impure, issue the principles and maxims that govern society. Law itself is but the reflex of homes. The tiniest bits of opinion sown in the minds of children in private life afterward issue forth to the world, and become its public opinion; for nations are gathered out of nurseries, and they who hold the leading strings of children may even exercise a greater power than those who wield the reins of government.

It is in the order of nature that domestic life should be preparatory to social, and that the mind and character should first be formed in the home. There the individuals who afterward form society are dealt with in detail, and fashioned one by one. From the family they enter life, and advance from boyhood to citizenship. Thus the home may be regarded as the most influential school of civilization. For, after all, civilization mainly resolves itself into a question of individual training; and according as the respective members of society are well or ill trained in youth, so will the community which they constitute be more or less humanized and civilized.

Thus homes, which are the nurseries of children who grow up into men and women, will be good or bad according to the power that governs them. Where the spirit of love and duty pervades the home--where head and heart bear rule wisely there--where the daily life is honest and virtuous--where the government is sensible, kind and loving, then may we expect from such a home an issue of healthy, useful, and happy beings, capable, as they gain the requisite strength of following the footsteps of their parents, of walking uprightly, governing themselves wisely, and contributing to the welfare of those about them.

On the other hand, if surrounded by ignorance, coarseness, and selfishness, they will unconsciously assume the same character, and grow up to adult years rude, uncultivated, and all the more dangerous to society if placed amidst the manifold temptations of what is called civilized life. "Give your child to be educated by a slave," said an ancient Greek, "and, instead of one slave, you will then have two."

The child cannot help imitating what he sees. Everything is to him a model--of manner, of gesture, of speech, of habit, of character. "For the child," says Richter, "the most important era of life is childhood, when he begins to color and mould himself by companionship with others. Every new educator effects less than his predecessor; until at last, if we regard all life as an educational institution, a circumnavigator of the world is less influenced by all the nations he has seen than by his nurse."

No man can select his parents or make for himself the early environment that affects character so powerfully, but he can found a home no matter how humble, at the outset, that will make his own future secure, as well as the future of those for whose existence he is responsible.

The poorest dwelling, presided over by a virtuous, thrifty, cheerful, and cleanly woman, may be the abode of comfort, virtue, and happiness; it may be the scene of every ennobling relation in family life; it may be endeared to a man by many delightful associations; furnishing a sanctuary for the heart, a refuge from the storms of life, a sweet resting-place after labor, a consolation in misfortune, a pride in prosperity, and a joy at all times.

The good home is the best of schools, not only in youth but in age. There young and old best learn cheerfulness, patience, self-control and the spirit of service and of duty. Isaak Walton, speaking of George Herbert's mother, says she governed the family with judicious care, not rigidly nor sourly, "but with such a sweetness and compliance with the recreations and pleasures of youth, as did incline them to spend much of their time in her company, which was to her great content."

The home is the true school of courtesy, of which woman is always the best practical instructor. "Without woman," says the Provencal proverb, "men were but ill-licked cubs." Philanthropy radiates from the home as from a centre. "To love the little platoon we belong to in society," said Burke "is the germ of all public affections." The wisest and the best have not been ashamed to own it to be their greatest joy and happiness to sit "behind the heads of the children" in the inviolable circle of home. A life of purity and duty there is not the least effectual preparative for a life of public work and duty; and the man who loves his home will not the less fondly love and serve his country.

At an address before a girls' school in Boston, ex-President John Quincy Adams, then an old man, said with much feeling: "As a child I enjoyed perhaps the greatest of blessings that can be bestowed upon man--that of a mother who was anxious and capable to form the characters of her children rightly. From her I derived whatever instruction (religious especially and moral) has pervaded a long life--I will not say perfectly, or as it ought to be; but I will say, because it is only justice to the memory of her I revere, that in the course of that life, whatever imperfection there has been or deviation from what she taught me, the fault is mine and not hers."

So much depends on the home, for it is the corner-stone of society and good government, that it is to be regretted, for the sake of young women, as well as of young men, that our modern life offers so many opportunities to neglect it.

As the home affects the character entirely through the associations, it follows that the young man who has left his home behind him should continue the associations whose memories comfort him. He should never go to a place for recreation where he would not be willing and proud to take his mother on his arm. He should never have as friends men to whom he would not be willing, if need be, to introduce his sister.

These are among the influences that help to success. But association is a matter of such great importance as to deserve fuller treatment.

CHAPTER IV
ASSOCIATION.

The old proverb, "Tell me your company and I will tell you what you are," is as true to-day as when first uttered. In the preparation for success, association is one of the most powerful factors, so powerful, indeed, that if the associations are not of the right kind, failure is inevitable.

As one diseased sheep may contaminate a flock, so one evil associate-- particularly if he be daring, may seriously injure the morals of many. Every young man can recall the evil influence of one bad boy on a whole school, but he cannot so readily point to the schoolmate, whose example and influence were for good; because goodness, though more potent, never makes itself so conspicuous as vice.

Criminals, preparing for the scaffold, have confessed that their entrance into a life of crime began in early youth, when the audacity of some unprincipled associate tempted them from the ways of innocence. Through all the years of life, even to old age, the life and character are influenced by association. If this be true in the case of the more mature and experienced, its force is intensified where the young, imaginative and susceptible, are concerned.

Man is said to be "an imitative animal." This is certainly true as to early education, and the tendency to imitate remains to a greater or less extent throughout life. Imitation is responsible for all the queer changes of fashion; and the desire to be "in the swim," as it is called, is entirely due to association.

In school days, the influence of a good home may counteract the effect of evil associates, whom the boy meets occasionally, but when the boy has grown to manhood, and finds himself battling with the world, away from home and well-tried friends, it is then that he is in the greatest danger from pernicious associates.

The young man who comes to the city to seek his fortune is more apt to be the victim of vile associates than the city raised youth whose experience of men is larger, and who is fortunate in his companionship. The farmer's son, who finds himself for the first time in a great city--alone and comparatively friendless, appears to himself to have entered a new world, as in truth he has. The crowds of hurrying, well-dressed people impress him forcibly as compared with his own clumsy gait, and roughly clad figure. The noise confuses him. The bustle of commerce amazes him; and for the time he is as desolate in feeling as if he were in the centre of a desert, instead of in the throbbing heart of a great city.

No matter how blessed with physical and mental strength the young man may be, under these circumstances he is very apt, for the time at least, to underestimate his own strength. He is powerfully impressed by what he deems the smartness or the superior manners of those whom he meets in his boarding house, or with whom he is associated in his business, say in a great mercantile establishment. It requires a great deal of moral courage for him to bear in a manly way the ridicule, covert or open, of the companions who regard him as a "hay-seed" or a "greenhorn." His Sunday clothes, which he wore with pride when he attended meeting with his mother, he is apt to regard with a feeling of mortification; and, perhaps, he secretly determines to dress as well as do his companions when he has saved enough money.

This is a crucial period in the life of every young man who is entering on a business career, and particularly so to him coming from the rural regions. He finds, perhaps, that his associates smoke or drink, or both; things which he has hitherto regarded with horror. He finds, too, they are in the habit of resorting to places of amusement, the splendor and mysteries of which arouse his curiosity, if not envy, as he hears them discussed.

Before leaving home, and while his mother's arms were still about him, he promised her to be moral and industrious, to write regularly, and to do nothing which she would not approve. If he had the right stuff in him, he would adhere manfully to the resolution made at the beginning; but, if he be weak or is tempted by false pride, or a prurient curiosity to "see the town," he is tottering on the edge of a precipice and his failure, if not sudden, is sure to come in time.

Cities are represented to be centres of vice, and it cannot be denied that the temptations in such places are much greater than on a farm or in a quiet country village, but at the same time, cities are centres of wealth and cultivation, places where philanthropy is alive and where organized effort has provided places of instruction and amusement for all young men, but particularly for that large class of youths who come from the country to seek their fortunes. Churches abound, and in connection with them there are societies of young people, organized for good work, which are ever ready, with open arms, to welcome the young stranger. Then, in all our cities and towns, there are to be found, branches of that most admirable institution, the Young Men's Christian Association. Not only are there companions to be met in these associations of the very best kind, but the buildings are usually fitted up with appliances for the improvement of mind and body. Here are gymnasiums, where strength and grace can be cultivated under the direction of competent teachers. Here are to be found well organized libraries. Here, particularly in the winter season, there are classes where all the branches of a high school are taught; and there are frequent lectures on all subjects of interest by the foremost teachers of the land.

If the young man falls under these influences, and he will experience not the slightest difficulty in doing so; indeed, he will find friendly hands extended to welcome and to help, the result on his character must be most beneficial. The clumsiness of rural life will soon depart; he will regard his home-made suit with as much pleasure as if it were made by a fashionable tailor, and he will soon learn to distinguish between the vicious and the virtuous, while he imitates the one and regards the other with indifference or contempt.

Next to the association of companions met in every day life nothing so powerfully influences the character of the young as association with good books, particularly those that relate to the lives of men who have struggled up to honor from small beginnings.

With such associations, and a capacity for honest persistent work, success is assured at the very threshold of effort.

CHAPTER V
COURAGE AND DETERMINED EFFORT.

Carlyle has said that the first requisite to success is carefully to find your life work and then bravely to carry it out. No soldier ever won a succession of triumphs, and no business man, no matter how successful in the end, who did not find his beginning slow, arduous and discouraging. Courage is a prime essential to prosperity. The young man's progress may be slow in comparison with his ambition, but if he keeps a brave heart and sticks persistently to it, he will surely succeed in the end.

The forceful, energetic character, like the forceful soldier on the battle-field, not only moves forward to victory himself, but his example has a stimulating influence on others.

Energy of character has always a power to evoke energy in others. It acts through sympathy, one of the most influential of human agencies. The zealous, energetic man unconsciously carries others along with him. His example is contagious and compels imitation. He exercises a sort of electric power, which sends a thrill through every fibre, flows into the nature of those about him, and makes them give out sparks of fire.

Dr. Arnold's biographer, speaking of the power of this kind exercised by him over young men, says: "It was not so much an enthusiastic admiration for true genius, or learning, or eloquence, which stirred the heart within them; it was a sympathetic thrill, caught from a spirit that was earnestly at work in the world--whose work was healthy, sustained and constantly carried forward in the fear of God--a work that was founded on a deep sense of its duty and its value."

The beginner should carefully study the lives of men whose undaunted courage has won in the face of obstacles that would cow weaker natures.

It is in the season of youth, while the character is forming, that the impulse to admire is the greatest. As we advance in life we crystallize into habit and "*Nil admirari*" too often becomes our motto. It is well to encourage the admiration of great characters while the nature is plastic and open to impressions; for if the good are not admired--as young men will have their heroes of some sort-- most probably the great bad may be taken by them for models. Hence it always rejoiced Dr. Arnold to hear his pupils expressing admiration of great deeds, or full of enthusiasm for persons or even scenery.

"I believe," said he, "that '*Nil admirari*' is the devil's favorite text; and he could not choose a better to introduce his pupils into the more esoteric parts of his doctrine. And therefore I have always looked upon a man infected with the disorder of anti-romance as one who has lost the finest part of his nature and his best protection against everything low and foolish."

Great men have evoked the admiration of kings, popes and emperors. Francis de Medicis never spoke to Michael Angelo without uncovering, and Julius III made him sit by his side while a dozen cardinals were standing. Charles V made way for Titian; and one day when the brush dropped from the painter's hand, Charles stooped and picked it up, saying, "You deserve to be served by an emperor."

Bear in mind that nothing so discourages or unfits a man for an effort as idleness. "Idleness," says Burton, in that delightful old book "The Anatomy of Melancholy," "is the bane of body and mind, the nurse of naughtiness, the chief mother of all mischief, one of the seven deadly sins, the devil's cushion, his pillow and chief reposal . . . An idle dog will be mangy; and how shall an idle person escape? Idleness of the mind is much worse than that of the body; wit, without employment, is a disease--the rust of the soul, a plague, a hell itself. As in a standing pool, worms and filthy creepers increase, so do evil and corrupt thoughts in an idle person; the soul is contaminated . . . Thus much I dare boldly say: he or she that is idle, be they of what condition they will, never so rich, so well allied, fortunate, happy--let them have all things in abundance, all felicity that heart can wish and desire, all contentment--so long as he, or she, or they, are idle, they shall never be pleased, never well in body or mind, but weary still, sickly still, vexed still, loathing still, weeping, sighing, grieving, suspecting, offended with the world, with every object, wishing themselves gone or dead, or else carried away with some foolish fantasy or other.".

Barton says a great deal more to the same effect.

It has been truly said that to desire to possess without being burdened by the trouble of acquiring is as much a sign of weakness as to recognize that everything worth having is only to be got by paying its price is the prime secret of practical strength. Even leisure cannot be enjoyed unless it is won by effort. If it have not been earned by work, the price has not been paid for it.

But apart from the supreme satisfaction of winning, the effort required to accomplish anything is ennobling, and, if there were no other success it would be its own reward.

"I don't believe," said Lord Stanley, in an address to the young men of Glasgow, "that an unemployed man, however amiable and otherwise respectable, ever was, or ever can be, really happy. As work is our life, show me what you can do, and I will show you what you are. I have spoken of love of one's work as the best preventive of merely low and vicious tastes. I will go farther and say that it is the best preservative against petty anxieties and the annoyances that arise out of indulged self-love. Men have thought before now that they could take refuge from trouble and vexation by sheltering themselves, as it wore, in a world of their own. The experiment has often been tried and always with one result. You cannot escape from anxiety or labor--it is the destiny of humanity . . . Those who shirk from facing trouble find that trouble comes to them.

"The early teachers of Christianity ennobled the lot of toil by their example. 'He that will not work,' said St. Paul, 'neither shall he eat;' and he glorified himself in that he had labored with his hands and had not been chargeable to any man. When St. Boniface landed in Britain, he came with a gospel in one hand, and a carpenter's rule in the other; and from England he afterward passed over into Germany, carrying thither the art of building. Luther also, in the midst of a multitude of other employments, worked diligently for a living, earning his bread by gardening, building, turning, and even clock-making."

Coleridge has truly observed, that "if the idle are described as killing time, the methodical man may be justly said to call it into life and moral being, while he makes it the distinct object, not only of the consciousness, but of the conscience. He organizes the hours and gives them a soul; and by that, the very essence of which is to fleet and to have been, he communicates an imperishable and spiritual nature.

Of the good and faithful servant, whose energies thus directed are thus method-
ized, it is less truly affirmed that he lives in time than that time lives in him. His
days and months and years, as the stops and punctual marks in the record of duties
performed, will survive the wreck of worlds, and remain extant when time itself
shall be no more."

Washington, also, was an indefatigable man of business. From his boyhood he
diligently trained himself in habits of application, of study and of methodical work.
His manuscript school-books, which are still preserved, show that, as early as the
age of thirteen, he occupied himself voluntarily, in copying out such things as forms
of receipts, notes of hand, bills of exchange, bonds, indentures, leases, land warrants
and other dry documents, all written out with great care. And the habits which
lie thus early acquired were, in a great measure the foundation of those admirable
business qualities which he afterward so successfully brought to bear in the affairs
of the government.

The man or woman who achieves success in the management of any great affair of business is entitled to honor--it may be, to as much as the artist who paints
a picture, or the author who writes a book, or the soldier who wins a battle. Their
success may have been gained in the face of as great difficulties, and after as great
struggles; and where they have won their battle it is at least a peaceful one and there
is no blood on their hands.

Courage, combined with energy and perseverance, will overcome difficulties
apparently insurmountable. It gives force and impulse to effort and does not permit
it to retreat. Tyndall said of Faraday, that "in his warm moments he formed a resolution and in his cool ones he made that resolution good." Perseverance, working in
the right direction, grows with time and when steadily practiced, even by the most
humble, will rarely fail of its reward. Trusting in the help of others is of comparatively little use. When one of Michael Angelo's principal patrons died, he said: "I
begin to understand the promises of the world are for the most part vain phantoms
and that to confide in one's self and become something of worth and value is the
best and safest course."

It ought to be a first principle, in beginning life to do with earnestness what
we have got to do. If it is worth doing at all, it is worth doing earnestly. If it is to be
done well at all it must be done with purpose and devotion.

Whatever may be our profession, let us mark all its bearings and details, its principles, its instruments, its applications. There is nothing about it should escape our study. There is nothing in it either too high or too low for our observation and knowledge. While we remain ignorant of any part of it, we are so far crippled in its use; we are liable to be taken at a disadvantage. This may be the very point the knowledge of which is most needed in some crisis, and those versed in it will take the lead, while we must be content to follow at a distance.

Our business, in short, must be the main drain of our intellectual activities day by day. It is the channel we have chosen for them they must follow in it with a diffusive energy, filling every nook and corner. This is a fair test of professional earnestness. When we find our thoughts running after our business, and fixing themselves with a familiar fondness upon its details, we may be pretty sure of our way. When we find them running elsewhere and only resorting with difficulty to the channel prepared for them, we may be equally sure we have taken a wrong turn. We cannot be earnest about anything which does not naturally and strongly engage our thoughts.

CHAPTER VI
THE IMPORTANCE OF CORRECT HABITS.

As has been stated, habit is the basis of character. Habit is the persistent repetition of acts physical, mental, and moral. No matter how much thought and ability a young man may have, failure is sure to follow bad habits. While correct habits depend largely on self- discipline, and often on self-denial, bad habits, like pernicious weeds, spring up unaided and untrained to choke out the plants of virtue. It is easy to destroy the seed at the beginning, but its growth is so rapid, that its evil effects may not be perceptible till the roots have sapped every desirable plant about it.

No sane youth ever started out with the resolve to be a thief, a tramp, or a drunkard. Yet it is the slightest deviation from honesty that makes the first. It is the first neglect of a duty that makes the second. And it is the first intoxicating glass that makes the third. It is so easy not to begin, but the habit once formed and the man is a slave, bound with galling, cankering chains, and the strength of will having been destroyed, only God's mercy can cast them off.

Next to the moral habits that are the cornerstone of every worthy character, the habit of industry should be ranked. In "this day and generation," there is a wild desire on the part of young men to leap into fortune at a bound, to reach the top of the ladder of success without carefully climbing the rounds, but no permanent prosperity was ever gained in this way.

There have been men, who through chance, or that form of speculation, that is legalized gambling, have made sudden fortunes; but as a rule these fortunes have been lost in the effort to double them by the quick and speculative process.

Betters and gamblers usually die poor. But even where young men have made a lucky stroke, the result is too often a misfortune. They neglect the necessary, persistent effort. The habit of industry is ignored. Work becomes distasteful, and the life is wrecked, looking for chances that never come.

There have been exceptional cases, where men of immoral habits, but with mental force and unusual opportunities have won fortunes. Some of these will come to the reader's mind at once, but he will be forced to confess that he would not give up his manhood and comparative poverty, in exchange for such material success.

The best equipment a young man can have for the battle of life is a conscience void of offense, sound common sense, and good health. Too much importance cannot be attached to health. It is a blessing we do not prize till it is gone. Some are naturally delicate and some are naturally strong, but by habit the health of the vigorous may be ruined, and by opposite habits the delicate may be made healthful and strong.

No matter the prospects and promises of overwork, it is a species of suicide to continue it at the expense of health. Good men in every department and calling, stimulated by zeal and an ambition commendable in itself, have worked till the vital forces were exhausted, and so were compelled to stop all effort in the prime of life and on the threshold of success.

The best preservers of health are regularity in correct hygienic habits, and strict temperance. Alexander Stephens, of Georgia, it is said contracted consumption when a child, and his friends did not believe he would live to manhood, yet by correct habits, he not only lived the allotted time of the Psalmist, but he did an amount of work that would have been impossible to a much stronger man, without his method of life.

It should not be forgotten that good health is quite as much dependent on mental as on physical habits. Worry, sensitiveness, and temper have hastened to the grave many an otherwise splendid character.

The man of business must needs be subject to strict rule and system. Business, like life, is managed by moral leverage; success in both depending in no small degree upon that regulation of temper and careful self-discipline, which give a wise man not only a command over himself, but over others. Forbearance and self-control smooth the road of life, and open many ways which would otherwise remain closed. And so does self-respect; for as men respect themselves, so will they usually, respect the personality of others.

It is the same in politics as in business. Success in that sphere of life is achieved less by talent than by temper, less by genius than by character. If a man have not self-control, he will lack patience, be wanting in tact, and have neither the power of governing himself nor managing others. When the quality most needed in a prime minister was the subject of conversation in the presence of Mr. Pitt, one of the speakers said it was "eloquence;" another said it was "knowledge;" and a third said it was "toil." "No," said Pitt, "it is patience!" And patience means self-control, a quality in which he himself was superb. His friend George Rose has said of him that he never once saw Pitt out of temper.

A strong temper is not necessarily a bad temper. But the stronger the temper, the greater is the need of self-discipline and self-control. Dr. Johnson says men grow better as they grow older, and improve with experience; but this depends upon the width and depth and generousness of their nature. It is not men's faults that ruin them so much as the manner in which they conduct themselves after the faults have been committed. The wise will profit by the suffering they cause, and eschew them for the future; but there are those on whom experience exerts no ripening influence, and who only grow narrower and bitterer, and more vicious with time.

What is called strong temper in a young man, often indicates a large amount of unripe energy, which will expend itself in useful work if the road be fairly opened to it. It is said of Girard that when he heard of a clerk with a strong temper, he would readily take him into his employment, and set him to work in a room by himself; Girard being of opinion that such persons were the best workers, and that their energy would expend itself in work if removed from the temptation of quarrel.

There is a great difference between a strong temper, "a righteous indignation," and that irritability that curses its possessor and all who come near him.

Mr. Motley compares William the Silent to Washington, whom he in many respects resembled. The American, like the Dutch patriot, stands out in history as the very impersonation of dignity, bravery, purity, and personal excellence. His command over his feelings, even in moments of great difficulty and danger, was such as to convey the impression, to those who did not know him intimately, that he was a man of inborn calmness and almost impassiveness of disposition. Yet Washington was by nature ardent and impetuous; his mildness, gentleness politeness, and consideration for others, were the result of rigid self-control and unwearied self-discipline, which he diligently practiced even from his boyhood. His biographer says of him, that "his temperament was ardent, his passions strong, and, amidst the multiplied scenes of temptation and excitement through which he passed, it was his constant effort, and ultimate triumph, to check the one and subdue the other." And again: "His passions were strong, and sometimes they broke out with vehemence, but he had the power of checking them in an instant. Perhaps self-control was the most remarkable trait of his character. It was in part the effect of discipline; yet he seems by nature to have possessed this power in a degree which has been denied to other men."

The Duke of Wellington's natural temper, like that of Napoleon, was strong in the extreme and it was only by watchful self-control that he was enabled to restrain it. He studied calmness and coolness in the midst of danger, like any Indian chief. At Waterloo, and elsewhere, he gave his orders in the most critical moments without the slightest excitement, and in a tone of voice almost more than usually subdued.

Abraham Lincoln in his early manhood was quick tempered and combative, but he soon learned self-control and, as all know, became as patient as he was forceful and sympathetic. "I got into the habit of controlling my temper in the Black Hawk war," he said to Colonel Forney, "and the good habit stuck to me as bad habits do to so many."

Patience is a habit that pays for its own cultivation and the biographies of earth's greatest men, prove that it was one of their most conspicuous characteristics.

One who loves right can not be indifferent to wrong, or wrong-doing. If he feels warmly, he will speak warmly, out of the fullness of his heart. We have, however, to be on our guard against impatient scorn. The best people are apt to have their impatient side, and often the very temper which makes men earnest, makes them also intolerant. "Of all mental gifts, the rarest is intellectual patience; and the last lesson of culture is to believe in difficulties which are invisible to ourselves."

One of Burns' finest poems, written in his twenty-eighth year, is entitled "A Bard's Epitaph." It is a description, by anticipation, of his own life. Wordsworth has said of it:

"Here is a sincere and solemn avowal; a public declaration from his own will; a confession at once devout, poetical, and human; a history in the shape of a prophecy." It concludes with these lines:

"Reader, attend--whether thy soul Soars fancy's flights beyond the pole, Or darkling grubs this earthly hole   In low pursuit; Know--prudent, cautious self-control,   Is Wisdom's root."

Truthfulness is quite as much a habit and quite as amendable to cultivation as falsehood. Deceit may meet with temporary success, but he who avails himself of it can be sure that in the end his "sin will find him out." The credit of the truthful, reliable man stands when the cash of a trickster might be doubted. "His word is as good as his bond," is one of the highest compliments that can be paid to the business man.

Be truthful not only in great things, but in all things. The slightest deviation from this habit may be the beginning of a career of duplicity, ending in disgrace.

But truthfulness, like the other virtues, should not be regarded as a trade mark, a means to success. It brings its own reward in the nobility it gives the character. An exception might be made here as to that form of military deceit known as "stratagem," but it is the duty of the enemy to expect it, and so guard against it. The word of a soldier involves his honor, and if he pledges that word, to even a foeman, he will keep it with his life.

Like our own Washington, Wellington was a severe admirer of truth. An illustration may be given. When afflicted by deafness, he consulted a celebrated aurist, who, after trying all remedies in vain, determined, as a last resource, to inject into the ear a strong solution of caustic. It caused the most intense pain, but the patient bore it with his usual equanimity. The family physician accidentally calling one day, found the duke with flushed cheeks and blood-shot eyes, and when he rose he staggered about like a drunken man. The doctor asked to be permitted to look at his ear, and then he found that a furious inflammation was going on, which, if not immediately checked, must shortly reach the brain and kill him. Vigorous remedies were at once applied, and the inflammation was checked. But the hearing of that ear was completely destroyed. When the aurist heard of the danger his patient had run, through the violence of the remedy he had employed, he hastened to Apsley

House to express his grief and mortification; but the duke merely said: "Do not say a word more about it--you did all for the best." The aurist said it would be his ruin when it became known that he had been the cause of so much suffering and danger to his grace. "But nobody need know any thing about it: keep your own counsel, and, depend upon it, I won't say a word to any one." "Then your grace will allow me to attend you as usual, which will show the public that you have not withdrawn your confidence from me?" "No," replied the duke, kindly but firmly; "I can't do that, for that would be a lie." He would not act a falsehood any more than he would speak one.

But lying assumes many forms--such as diplomacy, expediency, and moral reservation; and, under one guise or another, it is found more or less pervading all classes of society. Sometimes it assumes the form of equivocation or moral dodging--twisting and so stating the things said as to convey a false impression--a kind of lying which a Frenchman once described as "walking round about the truth."

There are even men of narrow minds and dishonest natures, who pride themselves upon their Jesuitical cleverness in equivocation, in their serpent-wise shirking of the truth and getting out of moral backdoors, in order to hide their real opinions and evade the consequences of holding and openly professing them. Institutions or systems based upon any such expedients must necessarily prove false and hollow. "Though a lie be ever so well dressed," says George Herbert, "it is ever overcome." Downright lying, though bolder and more vicious, is even less contemptible than such kind of shuffling and equivocation.

CHAPTER VII
AS TO MARRIAGE.

Mention has been made of the great influence on character of the right kind of a home, in childhood and youth. The right kind of a home depends almost entirely on the right kind of a wife or mother.

The old saying, "Marry in haste and repent at leisure," will never lose its force. "Worse than the man whose selfishness keeps him a bachelor till death, is the young man, who, under an impulse he imagines to be an undying love, marries a girl as poor, weak, and selfish as himself. There have been cases where marriage under such circumstances has aroused the man to effort and made him, particularly if his wife were of the same character, but these are so exceptional as to form no guide for people of average common sense.

Again, there have been men, good men, whose lives measured by the ordinary standards were successful, who never married; but those who hear or read of them, have the feeling that such careers were incomplete.

The most important voluntary act of every man and woman's life, is marriage, and God has so ordained it. Hence it is an act which should be love-prompted on both sides, and only entered into after the most careful and prayerful deliberation.

It is natural for young people of the opposite sex, who are much thrown together, and so become in a way essential to each other's happiness, to end by falling in love. It is said that "love is blind," and the ancients so painted their mythological god, Cupid. It is very certain that the fascination is not dependent on the will; it is a divine, natural impulse, which has for its purpose the continuance of the race.

Here, then, in all its force, we see the influence of association, which has been already treated of. The young man whose associations are of the right kind is sure to be brought into contact with the good daughters of good mothers. With such association, love and marriage should add to life's success and happiness, provided, always, that the husband's circumstances warrant him in establishing and maintaining a home.

Granting, then, the right kind of a wife, and the ability to make a home, the young man, with the right kind of stuff in him, takes a great stride in the direction of success when he marries.

No wise person will marry for beauty mainly. It may exercise a powerful attraction in the first place, but it is found to be of comparatively little consequence afterward. Not that beauty of person is to be underestimated, for, other things being equal, handsomeness of form and beauty of features are the outward manifestations of health. But to marry a handsome figure without character, fine features unbeautified by sentiment or good nature, is the most deplorable of mistakes. As even the finest landscape, seen daily, becomes monotonous, so does the most beautiful face, unless a beautiful nature shines through it. The beauty of to-day becomes commonplace to-morrow; whereas goodness, displayed through the most ordinary features, is perennially lovely. Moreover, this kind of beauty improves with age, and time ripens rather than destroys it. After the first year, married people rarely think of each other's features, whether they be classically beautiful or otherwise. But they never fail to be cognizant of each other's temper. "When I see a man," says Addison, "with a sour, riveted face, I can not forbear pitying his wife; and when I meet with an open, ingenuous countenance, I think of the happiness of his friends, his family, and his relations."

Edmund Burke, the greatest of English statesmen, was especially happy in his marriage. He never ceased to be a lover, and long years after the wedding he thus describes his wife: "She is handsome; but it is a beauty not arising from features, from complexion, or from shape. She has all three in a high degree, but it is not by these she touches the heart; it is all that sweetness of temper, benevolence, innocence, and sensibility, which a face can express, that forms her beauty. She has a face that just raises your attention at first sight; it grows on you every moment, and you wonder it did no more than raise your attention at first.

"Her eyes have a mild light, but they awe when she pleases; they command, like a good man out of office, not by authority, but by virtue.

"Her stature is not tall; she is not made to be the admiration of everybody, but the happiness of one.

"She has all the firmness that does not exclude delicacy; she has all the softness that does not imply weakness.

"Her voice is a soft, low music--not formed to rule in public assemblies, but to charm those who can distinguish a company from a crowd; it has this advantage--you must come close to her to hear it.

"To describe her body describes her mind--one is the transcript of the other; her understanding is not shown in the variety of matters it exerts itself on, but in the goodness of the choice she makes.

"She does not display it so much in saying or doing striking things, as in avoiding such as she ought not to say or do.

"No person of so few years can know the world better; no person was ever less corrupted by the knowledge of it."

A man's real character will always be more visible in his household than anywhere else; and his practical wisdom will be better exhibited by the manner in which he bears rule there than even in the larger affairs of business or public life. His whole mind may be in his business; but, if he would be happy, his whole heart must be in his home. It is there that his genuine qualities most surely display themselves--there that he shows his truthfulness, his love, his sympathy, his consideration for others, his uprightness, his manliness--in a word, his character. If affection be not the governing principle in a household, domestic life may be the most intolerable of despotisms. Without justice, also, there can be neither love, confidence, nor respect, on which all true domestic rule is founded.

It is by the regimen of domestic affection that the heart of man is best composed and regulated. The home is the woman's kingdom, her state, her world--where she governs by affection, by kindness, by the power of gentleness. There is nothing which so settles the turbulence of a man's nature as his union in life with a high-minded woman. There he finds rest, contentment, and happiness--rest of brain and peace of spirit. He will also often find in her his best counselor, for her instinctive tact will usually lead him right when his own unaided reason might be apt to go wrong. The true wife is a staff to lean upon in times of trial and difficulty; and she is never wanting in sympathy and solace when distress occurs or fortune frowns. In the time of youth, she is a comfort and an ornament of man's life; and she remains a faithful helpmate in maturer years, when life has ceased to be an anticipation, and we live in its realities.

Luther, a man full of human affection, speaking of his wife, said, "I would not exchange my poverty with her for all the riches of Croesus without her." Of marriage he observed: "The utmost blessing that God can confer on a man is the possession of a good and pious wife, with whom he may live in peace and tranquility--to whom he may confide his whole possessions, even his life and welfare." And again he said, "To rise betimes, and to marry young, are what no man ever repents of doing."

Some persons are disappointed in marriage, because they expect too much from it; but many more because they do not bring into the co- partnership their fair share of cheerfulness, kindliness, forbearance, and common sense. Their imagination has perhaps pictured a condition never experienced on this side of heaven; and when real life comes, with its troubles and cares, there is a sudden waking-up as from a dream.

We have spoken of the influence of a wife upon a man's character. There are few men strong enough to resist the influence of a lower character in a wife. If she do not sustain and elevate what is highest in his nature, she will speedily reduce him to her own level. Thus a wife may be the making or the unmaking of the best of men. An illustration of this power is furnished in the life of Bunyan, the profligate tinker, who had the good fortune to marry, in early life, a worthy young woman, of good parentage.

On hearing of the death of his wife, the great explorer, Dr. Livingstone, wrote to a friend: "I must confess that this heavy stroke quite takes the heart out of me. Every thing else that has happened only made me more determined to overcome all difficulties; but after this sad stroke I feel crushed and void of strength. Only three short months of her society, after four years' separation! I married her for love, and the longer I lived with her I loved her the more. A good wife, and a good, brave, kind-hearted mother was she, deserving all the praises you bestowed upon her at our parting dinner, for teaching her own and the native children, too, at Kolobeng. I try to bow to the blow as from our Heavenly Father, who orders all things for us . . . I shall do my duty still, but it is with a darkened horizon that I again set about it."

Besides being a helper, woman is emphatically a consoler. Her sympathy is unfailing. She soothes, cheers, and comforts. Never was this more true than in the case of the wife of Tom Hood, whose tender devotion to him, during a life that was a prolonged illness, is one of the most affecting things in biography. A woman of excellent good sense, she appreciated her husband's genius, and, by encouragement and sympathy, cheered and heartened him to renewed effort in many a weary struggle for life. She created about him an atmosphere of hope and cheerfulness, and nowhere did the sunshine of her love seem so bright as when lighting up the couch of her invalid husband.

Scott wrote beautifully and truthfully:

"Oh, woman, in our hours of ease,   Uncertain, coy, and hard to please,   And variable as the shade   By the light, quivering aspen made,   When pain and anguish wring the brow,   A ministering angel thou."

CHAPTER VIII
EDUCATION AS DISTINGUISHED FROM LEARNING.

Although not the same kind, there is as much difference between education and learning, as there is between character and reputation.

Learning may be regarded as mental capital, in the way of accumulated facts. Education is the drawing out and development of the best that is in the heart, the head, and the hand.

The civilized world has a score of very learned men, to the one who may be said to be thoroughly educated. The learned man may be familiar with many languages, and sciences, and have all the facts of history and literature at his fingers' tip, and yet be as helpless as an infant and as impractical as a fool. An educated man, a man with his powers developed by training, may know no language but his mother tongue, may be ignorant as to literature and art, and yet be well--yes, even superbly educated.

The learned man's mind may be likened to a store house, or magazine, in which there are a thousand wonderful things, some of which he can make of use in the battle of life. He resembles the miser who fills his coffers with gold and keeps it out of circulation. Beyond the selfish joy of possession, his wealth is worthless, and its acquisition has unfitted him for the struggle. The educated man, to continue the illustration, may not be rich, but he knows how to use every cent he owns, and he places it where, under his energy, it will grow into dollars.

Far be it from us to underestimate the value of learning. Many of the world's greatest men have been learned, but without exception such men have also been educated. They have been trained to make their knowledge available for the benefit of themselves and their fellow men.

The athlete who develops his muscles to their greatest capacity of strength and flexibility, and this can only be done by observing strictly the laws of health, is physically an educated man. Every mechanic whose hands and brain have been trained to the expertness required by the master workman, is well-educated in his particular calling. The man who is an expert accountant, or a trained civil engineer, may know nothing of the higher mathematical principles, but he is better educated than the scholar who has only a theoretical knowledge of all the mathematics that have ever been published.

The educated man is the man who can do something, and the quality of his work marks the degree of his education. One might be learned in law in a phenomenal way, and yet, unless he was educated, trained to the practice, he would be beaten in the preparation of a case by a lawyer's clerk.

There are men who can write and talk learnedly on political economy and the laws of trade, and quote from memory all the statistics of the census library, and yet be immeasurably surpassed in practical business, by a young man whose college was the store, and whose university was the counting room.

It should not be inferred from this that learning is not of the greatest value, or that the facts obtained from the proper books are to be ignored. The best investment a young man can make is in good books, the study of which broadens the mind, and the facts of which equip him the better for his life calling.

But books are not valuable only because of the available information they give; when they do not instruct, they elevate and refine.

"Books," said Hazlitt, "wind into the heart; the poet's verse slides into the current of our blood. We read them when young, we remember them when old. We read there of what has happened to others; we feel that it has happened to ourselves. They are to be had everywhere cheap and good. We breathe but the air of books. We owe everything to their authors, on this side barbarism."

A good book is often the best urn of a life, enshrining the best thoughts of which that life was capable; for the world of a man's life is, for the most part, but the world of his thoughts. Thus the best books are treasuries of good words and golden thoughts, which, remembered and cherished, become our abiding companions and comforters. "They are never alone," said Sir Philip Sidney, "that are accompanied by noble thoughts." The good and true thought may in time of temptation be as an angel of mercy, purifying and guarding the soul. It also enshrines the germs of action, for good words almost invariably inspire to good works.

Thus Sir Henry Lawrence prized above all other compositions Wordsworth's "Character of the Happy Warrior," which he endeavored to embody in his own life. It was ever before him as an exemplar. He thought of it continually, and often quoted it to others. His biographer says, "He tried to conform his own life and to assimilate his own character to it; and he succeeded, as all men succeed who are truly in earnest."

Books possess an essence of immortality. They are by far the most lasting products of human effort. Temples crumble into ruin; pictures and statues decay; but books survive. Time is of no account with great thoughts, which are as fresh to-day as when they first passed through their authors' minds, ages ago. What was then said and thought still speaks to us as vividly as ever from the printed page. The only effect of time has been to sift and winnow out the bad products; for nothing in literature can long survive but what is really good.

To the young man, "thirsting for learning and hungering for education," there are no books more helpful than the biographies of those whom it is well to imitate. Longfellow wisely says:

"Lives of great men all remind us,   We can make our lives sublime, And departing leave behind us,   Footprints on the sands of time--

 Footprints which perhaps another,   Sailing o'er life's solemn main, A forlorn and ship-wrecked brother,   Seeing, may take heart again."

At the head of all biographies stands the Great Biography--the Book of Books. And what is the Bible, the most sacred and impressive of all books--the educator of youth, the guide of manhood, and the consoler of age--but a series of biographies of great heroes and patriarchs, prophets, kings and judges, culminating in the greatest biography of all--the Life embodied in the New Testament? How much have the great examples there set forth done for mankind! How many have drawn from them their best strength, their highest wisdom, their best nurture and admonition! Truly does a great and deeply pious writer describe the Bible as a book whose words "live in the ear like a music that never can be forgotten--like the sound of church-bells which the convert hardly knows how he can forego. Its felicities often seem to be almost things rather than mere words. It is part of the national mind, and the anchor of national seriousness. The memory of the dead passes into it. The potent traditions of childhood are stereotyped in its verses. The power of all the griefs and trials of man is hidden beneath its words. It is the representative of his best moments; and all that has been about him of soft, and gentle, and pure, and penitent, and good, speaks to him forever out of his English Bible. It is his sacred thing, which doubt has never dimmed and controversy never soiled. In the length and breadth of the land there is not an individual with one spark of religiousness about him whose spiritual biography is not in his Saxon Bible."

History itself is best studied in biography. Indeed, history is biography--collective humanity as influenced and governed by individual men. "What is all history," says Emerson, "but the work of ideas, a record of the incomparable energy which his infinite aspirations infuse into man? In its pages it is always persons we see more than principles. Historical events are interesting to us mainly in connection with the feelings, the sufferings, and interests of those by whom they are accomplished. In history we are surrounded by men long dead, but whose speech and whose deeds survive. We almost catch the sound of their voices; and what they did constitutes the interest of history. We never feel personally interested in masses of men; but we feel and sympathize with the individual actors, whose biographies afford the finest and most real touches in all great historical dramas."

As in portraiture, so in biography--there must be light and shade. The portrait-painter does not pose his sitter so as to bring out his deformities; nor does the biographer give undue prominence to the defects of the character he portrays. Not many men are so outspoken as Cromwell was when he sat to Cooper for his miniature: "Paint me as I am," said he, "wart and all." Yet, if we would have a faithful likeness of faces and characters, they must be painted as they are. "Biography," said Sir Walter Scott, "the most interesting of every species of composition, loses all its interest with me when the shades and lights of the principal characters are not accurately and faithfully detailed. I can no more sympathize with a mere eulogist than I can with a ranting hero on the stage."

It is to be regretted that in this day the country is flooded with cheap, trashy fiction, the general tendency of which is not only not educational, but is positively destructive. The desire to read this stuff is as demoralizing as the opium habit.

There are works of fiction, cheap and available, too, whose influence is elevating, and some knowledge of which is essential to the young man who is using his spare hours for the purpose of self-education.

There is no room for doubt that the surpassing interest which fiction, whether in poetry or prose, possesses for most minds arises mainly from the biographic element which it contains. Homer's "Iliad "owes its marvelous popularity to the genius which its author displayed in the portrayal of heroic character. Yet he does not so much describe his personages in detail as make them develop themselves by their actions. "There are in Homer," said Dr. Johnson, "such characters of heroes and combination of qualities of heroes, that the united powers of mankind ever since have not produced any but what are to be found there."

The genius of Shakespeare, also, was displayed in the powerful delineation of character, and the dramatic evolution of human passions. His personages seem to be real--living and breathing before us. So, too, with Cervantes, whose Sancho Panza, though homely and vulgar, is intensely human. The characters in Le Sage's "Gil Bias," in Goldsmith's "Vicar of Wakefield," and in Scott's marvelous muster-roll, seem to us almost as real as persons whom we have actually known; and De Foe's greatest works are but so many biographies, painted in minute detail, with reality so apparently stamped upon every page that it is difficult to believe his Robinson Crusoe and Colonel Jack to have been fictitious persons instead of real ones.

Then we have a fine American literature, which should be read after the history of the country is mastered, the stories of Cooper are fresh and invigorating, and those of Hawthorne are life studies and prose poems. Holmes, Lowell, Emerson, Bayard Taylor, and scores of other American writers, whose pens have added lustre to the country, will well repay the reader.

Good books are among the best of companions; and, by elevating the thoughts and aspirations, they act as preservatives against low associations. "A natural turn for reading and intellectual pursuits," says Thomas Hood, "probably preserved me from the moral ship-wreck so apt to befall those who are deprived in early life of their parental pilotage. My books kept me from the ring, the dogpit, the tavern, the saloon. The closet associate of Pope and Addison, the mind accustomed to the noble though silent discourse of Shakespeare and Milton, will hardly seek or put up with low company and slaves."

It has been truly said that the best books are those which most resemble good actions. They are purifying, elevating, and sustaining; they enlarge and liberalize the mind; they preserve it against vulgar worldliness; they tend to produce high-minded cheerfulness and equanimity of character; they fashion, and shape, and humanize the mind. In the Northern universities, the schools in which the ancient classics are studied are appropriately styled "The Humanity Classes."

Erasmus, the great scholar, was even of opinion that books were the necessaries of life, and clothes the luxuries; and he frequently postponed buying the latter until he had supplied himself with the former. His greatest favorites were the writings of Cicero, which he says he always felt himself the better for reading. "I can never," he says, "read the works of Cicero on 'Old Age,' or 'Friendship,' or his 'Tusculan Disputations,' without fervently pressing them to my lips, without being penetrated with veneration for a mind little short of inspired by God himself."

It is unnecessary to speak of the enormous moral influence which books have exercised upon the general civilization of mankind, from the Bible downward. They contain the treasured knowledge of the human race. They are the record of all labors, achievements, speculations, successes, and failures, in science, philosophy, religion, and morals. They have been the greatest motive-powers in all times. "From the Gospel to the Contrat Social," says De Bonald, "it is books that have made revolutions." Indeed, a great book is often a greater thing than a great battle. Even works of fiction have occasionally exercised immense power on society.

Bear in mind that it is not all we eat that nourishes, but what we digest. The learned man is a glutton as to books, but the educated man knows that, no matter how much is read, benefit is only derived from the thoughts that develop our own thoughts and strengthen our own minds.

CHAPTER IX
THE VALUE OF EXPERIENCE.

W hat experience have you had?" This is apt to be the first question put by an employer to the applicant for a place, be he mechanic, clerk, or laborer. If you need a doctor, you would prefer to trust your case to a man of experience, rather than to one fresh from a medical college. Apart from the established reputation, that comes only with time, and natural abilities which count for much, the principal difference between men in every calling is the difference in their experiences.

If this experience is so essential, we must regard as wanting in judgment the young man, who, after a short service, imagines he is as well qualified to conduct the business as his superior in place. No amount of natural ability, and no effort of energy can compensate for the training that comes from experience. Indeed, it is only after we have studied and tested ourselves, and overestimated our talents to our injury, more than once, that experience gives us a proper estimate of our own strength and weakness.

Contact with others is requisite to enable a man to know himself. It is only by mixing freely in the world that one can form a proper estimate of his own capacity. Without such experience, one is apt to become conceited, puffed up, and arrogant; at all events, he will remain ignorant of himself, though he may heretofore have enjoyed no other company.

Swift once said: "It is an uncontroverted truth, that no man ever made an ill-figure who understood his own talents, nor a good one who mistook them." Many persons, however, are readier to take measure of the capacity of others than of themselves. "Bring him to me," said a certain Dr. Tronchin, of Geneva, speaking of Rousseau-- "bring him to me that I may see whether he has got anything in him!"-

-the probability being that Rousseau, who knew himself better, was much more likely to take measure of Tronchin than Tronchin was to take measure of him.

A due amount of self-knowledge is, therefore, necessary for those who would *be* anything or *do* anything in the world. It is also one of the first essentials to the formation of distinct personal convictions. Frederick Perthes once said to a young friend, "You know only too well what you *can* do; but till you have learned what you *can not* do, you will neither accomplish anything of moment nor know inward peace."

Any one who would profit by experience will never be above asking help. He who thinks himself already too wise to learn of others, will never succeed in doing anything either good or great. We have to keep our minds and hearts open, and never be ashamed to learn, with the assistance of those who are wiser and more experienced than ourselves.

The man made wise by experience endeavors to judge correctly of the things which come under his observation and form the subject of his daily life. What we call common sense is, for the most part, but the result of common experience wisely improved. Nor is great ability necessary to acquire it, so much as patience, accuracy, and watchfulness.

The results of experience are, of course, only to be achieved by living; and living is a question of time. The man of experience learns to rely upon time as his helper. "Time and I against any two," was a maxim of Cardinal Mazarin. Time has been described as a beautifier and as a consoler; but it is also a teacher. It is the food of experience, the soil of wisdom. It may be the friend or the enemy of youth; and time will sit beside the old as a consoler or as a tormentor, according as it has been used or misused, and the past life has been well or ill spent.

"Time," says George Herbert, "is the rider that breaks youth." To the young, how bright the new world looks!--how full of novelty, of enjoyment, of pleasure! But as years pass, we find the world to be a place of sorrow as well as of joy. As we proceed through life, many dark vistas open upon us--of toil, suffering, difficulty, perhaps misfortune and failure. Happy they who can pass through and amidst such trials with a firm mind and pure heart, encountering trials with cheerfulness, and standing erect beneath even the heaviest burden!

Thomas A. Edison, the great inventor, in speaking of his success to the writer, said:

"I had when I started out all the patience and perseverance that I have now, but I lacked the experience. Seeing that I had only ten weeks' regular schooling in all my life, I can say with truth that experience has been my school and my only one.

"Many believe that my life has been a success from the start, and I do not try to undeceive them, but as a matter of fact my failures have exceeded my successes as one hundred to one; but even the experience of these failures has been in itself an educator and has enabled me not to repeat them."

The brave man will not be baffled, but tries and tries again until he succeeds. The tree does not fall at the first stroke, but only by repeated strokes and after great labor. We may see the visible success at which a man has arrived, but forget the toil and suffering and peril through which it has been achieved. For the same reason, it is often of advantage for a man to be under the necessity of having to struggle with poverty and conquer it. "He who has battled," says Carlyle, "were it only with poverty and hard toil, will be found stronger and more expert than he who could stay at home from the battle, concealed among the provision wagons, or even rest unwatchfully 'abiding by the stuff.'"

Scholars have found poverty tolerable compared with the privation of intellectual food. Riches weigh much more heavily upon the mind. "I cannot but choose say to Poverty," said Richter, "Be welcome! So that thou come not too late in life." Poverty, Horace tells us, drove him to poetry and poetry introduced him to Varus and Virgil and Maecenas. "Obstacles," says Michelet, "are great incentives. I lived for whole years upon a Virgil and found myself well off."

Many have to make up their minds to encounter failure again and again before they succeed; but if they have pluck, the failure will only serve to rouse their courage and stimulate them to renewed efforts. Talma, the greatest of actors, was hissed off the stage when he first appeared on it. Lacordaire, one of the greatest preachers of modern times, only acquired celebrity after repeated failures. Montalembert said of his first public appearance in the church of St. Roch: He failed completely, and, on coming out, every one said, "Though he may be a man of talent he will never be a preacher." Again and again he tried, until he succeeded, and only two years after his *debut*, Lacordaire was preaching in Notre Dame to audiences such as few French orators have addressed since the time of Bossuet and Massilon.

When Mr. Cobden first appeared as a speaker at a public meeting in Manchester, he completely broke down and the chairman apologized for his failure. Sir James Graham and Mr. Disraeli failed and were derided at first, and only succeeded by dint of great labor and application. At one time Sir James Graham had almost given up public speaking in despair. He said to his friend Sir Francis Baring: "I have tried it every way--extempore, from notes, and committing it all to memory--and I can't do it. I don't know why it is, but I am afraid I shall never succeed." Yet by dint of perseverance, Graham, like Disraeli, lived to become one of the most effective and impressive of parliamentary speakers.

In every field of effort success has only come after many trials. Morse with his telegraph and Howe with his sewing machine lived in poverty and met with many disappointments before the world came to appreciate the value of their great inventions.

It can be said with truth that these great men could have avoided much of their trouble if they had had the necessary experience. But particularly in the two cases cited before, the inventions were new to the world and it needed that the world should have the experience of their utility as well as the inventors.

Science also has had its martyrs, who have fought their way to light through difficulty, persecution and suffering. We need not refer to the cases of Bruno, Galileo and others, persecuted because of the supposed heterodoxy of their views. But there have been other unfortunates among men of science, whose genius has been unable to save them from the fury of their enemies. Thus Bailly, the celebrated French astronomer (who had been mayor of Paris) and Lavoisier, the great chemist, were both guillotined in the first French Revolution. When the latter, after being sentenced to death by the Commune, asked for a few days' respite to enable him to ascertain the result of some experiments he had made during his confinement, the tribunal refused his appeal, and ordered him for immediate execution, one of the judges saying that "the Republic has no need of philosophers." In England also, about the same time, Dr. Priestley, the father of modern chemistry, had his house burned over his head and his library destroyed, amidst the shouts of "No philosophers!" and he fled from his native country to lay his bones in a foreign land.

Courageous men have often turned enforced solitude to account in executing works of great pith and moment. It is in solitude that the passion for spiritual perfection best nurses itself. The soul communes with itself in loneliness until its energy often becomes intense. But whether a man profits by solitude or not will mainly depend upon his own temperament, training and character. While, in a large-natured man, solitude will make the pure heart purer, in the small-natured man it will only serve to make the hard heart still harder; for though solitude may be the nurse of great spirits, it is the torment of small ones.

Not only have many of the world's greatest benefactors, men whose lives history now records the most successful, had not only to contend with poverty, but it was their misfortune to be misunderstood and to be regarded as criminals. Many a great reformer in religion, science, and government has paid for his opinions by imprisonment. Speaking of these great men, a prominent English writer says: Prisons may have held them, but their thoughts were not to be confined by prison walls. They have burst through and defied the power of their persecutors. It was Lovelace, a prisoner, who wrote:

"Stone walls do not a prison make,   Nor iron bars a cage; Minds innocent and quiet take   That for a hermitage."

It was a saying of Milton that, "who best can suffer, best can do." The work of many of the greatest men, inspired by duty, has been done amidst suffering and trial and difficulty. They have struggled against the tide and reached the shore exhausted, only to grasp the sand and expire. They have done their duty and been content to die. But death hath no power over such men; their hallowed memories still survive to soothe and purify and bless us. "Life," said Goethe, "to us all is suffering. Who save God alone shall call us to our reckoning? Let not reproaches fall on the departed. Not what they have failed in, nor what they have suffered, but what they have done, ought to occupy the survivors."

Thus, it is not ease and facility that try men and bring out the good that is in them, so much as trial and difficulty. Adversity is the touchstone of character. As some herbs need to be crushed to give forth their sweetest odor, so some natures need to be tried by suffering to evoke the excellence that is in them. Hence trials often unmask virtues and bring to light hidden graces.

Suffering may be the appointed means by which the higher nature of man is to be disciplined and developed. Assuming happiness to be the end of being, sorrow may be the indispensable condition through which it is to be reached. Hence St.

Paul's noble paradox descriptive of the Christian life--"As chastened, and not killed; as sorrowful, yet always rejoicing; as poor, yet making many rich; as having nothing, and yet possessing all things."

Even pain is not all painful. On one side it is related to suffering, and on the other to happiness. For pain is remedial as well as sorrowful. Suffering is a misfortune as viewed from the one side, and a discipline as viewed from the other. But for suffering, the best part of many men's natures would sleep a deep sleep. Indeed, it might almost be said that pain and sorrow were the indispensable conditions of some men's success, and the necessary means to evoke the highest development of their genius. Shelley has said of poets:

"Most wretched men are cradled into poetry   by wrong, They learn in suffering what they teach in   song."

But the young man meeting with disappointments, as he is sure to do in the beginning of his career, particularly if he be dependent on himself, should take comfort from the thought that others who have risen to success have had to travel the same hard road; and such men have confessed that these trials, these bitter experiences, were the most valuable of their lives.

Life, all sunshine without shade, all happiness without sorrow, all pleasure without pain, were not life at all--at least not human life. Take the lot of the happiest--it is a tangled yarn. It is made up of sorrows and joys; and the joys are all the sweeter because of the sorrows; bereavements and blessings, one following another, making us sad and blessed by turns. Even death itself makes life more loving; it binds us more closely together while here. Dr. Thomas Browne has argued that death is one of the necessary conditions of human happiness, and he supports his argument with great force and eloquence. But when death comes into a household, we do not philosophize--we only feel. The eyes that are full of tears do not see; though in course of time they come to see more clearly and brightly than those that have never known sorrow.

There is much in life that, while in this state, we can never comprehend. There is, indeed, a great deal of mystery in life--much that we see "as in a glass darkly." But though we may not apprehend the full meaning of the discipline of trial through which the best have to pass, we must have faith in the completeness of the design of which our little individual lives form a part.

We have each to do our duty in that sphere of life in which we have been placed. Duty alone is true; there is no true action but in its accomplishment. Duty is the end and aim of the highest life; the truest pleasure of all is that derived from the consciousness of its fulfillment. Of all others, it is the one that is most thoroughly satisfying, and the least accompanied by regret and disappointment. In the words of George Herbert, the consciousness of duty performed "gives us music at midnight."

And when we have done our work on earth--of necessity, of labor, of love, or of duty--like the silk-worm that spins its little cocoon and dies, we too depart. But, short though our stay in life may be, it is the appointed sphere in which each has to work out the great aim and end of his being to the best of his power; and when that is done, the accidents of the flesh will affect but little the immortality we shall at last put on.

CHAPTER X
SELECTING A CALLING.

In reading the lives of great men, one is struck with a very important fact: that their success has been won in callings for which in early manhood they had no particular liking. Necessity or chance has, in many cases, decided what their life-work should be. But even where the employment was at first uncongenial, a strict sense of duty and a strong determination to master the difficult and to like the disagreeable, conquered in the end.

In these days of fierce competition, no matter how ardent the desire for fame, he is a dreamer who loses sight of the monetary returns of his life-efforts.

There have been a few men whose wants were simple, and these wants guarded against by a certain official income, who could afford to ignore gain and to work for the truths of science or the good of humanity. The great English chemist Faraday was of this class. Once asked by a friend why he did not use his great abilities and advantages to accumulate a fortune, he said: "My dear fellow, I haven't time to give to money making."

It is, perhaps, to be regretted that in nearly every case the efforts of to-day, whether in commerce, trade, or science, have for their purpose the making of fortunes. Nor should this spirit be condemned, for fortune in the hands of the right men is a blessing to the world and particularly to those who are more improvident.

Peter Cooper, Stephen Girard, George Peabody, and many other eminent Americans who made their way to great wealth from comparative poverty, used that wealth to enable young men, starting life as they did, to achieve the same success without having to encounter the same obstacles.

It is a well-known fact that boys who live near the sea have an intense yearning to become sailors. Every healthy boy has a longing to be a soldier, and he takes the greatest delight in toy military weapons.

Our ideals for living, particularly when they are the creations of a youthful imagination, are but seldom safe guides for our mature years. The fairy stories that delighted our childhood and the romances that fired our youth, are found but poor guides to success, when the great life-battle is on us.

It is a mistake for parents and guardians to say that this boy or that girl shall follow out this or that life-calling, without any regard to the tastes, or any consideration of the natural capacity. It is equally an error, because the boy or girl may like this or that branch of study more than another, to infer that this indicates a talent for that subject. Arithmetic is but seldom as popular with young people as history, simply because the latter requires less mental effort to master it. The world is full of professional incompetents--creatures of circumstances very often, but more frequently their life-failure is due to the whims of ambitious parents.

While the child and even the young man are but seldom the best judges of what a life-calling should be, yet the observant parent and teacher can discover the natural inclination, and by encouragement, develop this inclination.

As the wrecks on sandy beaches and by rock-bound shores, warn the careful mariner from the same fate, so the countless wrecks which the young man sees on every hand, increasing as he goes through life, should warn him from the same dangers.

It is stated, on what seems good authority, that ninety-five percent of the men who go into business for themselves, fail at some time. It would be an error, however, to infer from this that the failures were due to a mistaken life-calling. They have been due rather to unforeseen circumstances, over-confidence, or the desire to succeed too rapidly. Benefiting by these reverses, a large percent of the failures have entered on the life-struggle again and won.

In the early days of the world's history, the callings or fields of effort were necessarily limited to the chase, herding or agriculture. In those times, the toiler had not only to work for the support of himself and family, but he had also to be a warrior, trained to the use of arms, and ready to defend the products of his labor from the theft of robber neighbors.

In this later and broader day, civilization has opened up thousands of avenues of effort that were unknown to our less fortunate ancestors.

While the world is filled with human misfits, round pegs in square holes and square pegs in round holes, the choice of callings has so spread with the growth of civilization, that every young man who reasons for himself and studies his own powers, can with more or less certainty find out his calling, and pursue it with a success entirely dependent on his own fitness and energy.

In a general way, the great fields of human effort, at this time, may be divided into three classes. First, the so-called "learned professions"--journalism, theology, medicine and law. Second, the callings pertaining to public life, such as politics, military, science, and education. Third, those vocations that pertain to production, like agriculture, manufactures, and commerce.

But apart from the callings selected, it should be kept carefully in mind that, no matter the business, success is dependent entirely on the man.

Business is the salt of life, which not only gives a grateful smack to it, but dries up those crudities that would offend, preserves from putrefaction, and drives off all those blowing flies that would corrupt it. Let a man be sure to drive his business rather than let it drive him. When a man is but once brought to be driven, he becomes a vassal to his affairs. Reason and right give the quickest dispatch. All the entanglements that we meet with arise from the irrationality of ourselves or others. With a wise and honest man a business is soon ended, but with a fool and knave there is no conclusion, and seldom even a beginning.

Having decided on a calling, bear ever in mind that faith and trustfulness lie at the foundation of trade and commercial intercourse, and business transactions of every kind. A community of known swindlers and knaves would try in vain to avail themselves of the advantages of traffic, or to gain access to those circles where honor and honesty are indispensable passports. Hence the value which is attached, by all right-minded men, to purity of purpose and integrity of character. A man may be unfortunate, he may be poor and penniless; but if he is known to possess unbending integrity, an unwavering purpose to do what is honest and just, he will have friends and patrons whatever may be the embarrassments and exigencies into which he is thrown. The poor man may thus possess a capital of which none of the misfortunes and calamities of life can deprive him. We have known men who have been suddenly reduced from affluence to penury by misfortunes, which they could neither foresee nor prevent. A fire has swept away the accumulations of years; misplaced confidence, a flood, or some of the thousand casualties to which commercial men are exposed, have stripped them of their possessions. To-day they have been prosperous, to-morrow every prospect is blighted, and everything in its aspect is dark and dismal. Their business is gone, their property is gone, and they feel that all is gone; but they have a rich treasure which the fire cannot consume, which the flood cannot carry away. They have integrity of character, and this gives them influence, raises up friends, and furnishes them with means to start afresh in the world once more. Young men, especially, should be deeply impressed with the vast importance of cherishing those principles, and of cultivating those habits, which will secure for them the confidence and esteem of the wise and good. Let it be borne in mind that no brilliancy of genius, no tact or talent in business, and no amount of success, will compensate for duplicity, shuffling, and trickery. There may be apparent advantage in the art and practice of dissimulation, and in violating those great principles which lie at the foundation of truth and duty; but it will at length be seen that a dollar was lost where a cent was gained; that present successes are outweighed, a thousand-fold, by the pains and penalties which result from loss of confidence and loss of reputation. It cannot be too strongly impressed upon the minds of young men to abstain from every course, from every act, which shocks their moral sensibilities, wounds their conscience, and has a tendency to weaken their sense of honor and integrity.

CHAPTER XI
WE MUST HELP OURSELVES.

To the young man of the right kind, the inheritance of a fortune, or the possession of influential friends, may be great advantages, but more frequently they are hindrances. To win you must fight for yourself, and the effort will give you strength.

The spirit of self-help is the root of all genuine growth in the individual; and, exhibited in the lives of many, it constitutes the true source of national vigor and strength. Help from without is often enfeebling in its effects, but help from within invariably invigorates. Whatever is done *for* men or classes, to a certain extent takes away the stimulus and necessity of doing for themselves; and where men are subjected to over-guidance and over- government, the inevitable tendency is to render them comparatively helpless.

The privileges of a superior education, like the inheritance of a fortune, depends upon the man. It should encourage those who have only themselves and God to look to for support, to remember that self-education is the best education, and that some of the greatest men have had few or no school advantages.

Daily experience shows that it is energetic individualism which produces the most powerful effects upon the life and action of others, and really constitutes the best practical education. Schools, academies, and colleges give but the merest beginnings of culture in comparison with it. Far more influential is the life- education daily given in our homes, in the streets, behind counters, in workshops, at the loom and the plough, in counting-houses and manufactories, and in the busy haunts of men. This is that finishing instruction as members of society, which Schiller designated "the education of the human race," consisting in action, conduct, self- culture, self-control--all that tends to discipline a man truly, and fit him for the proper performance of the duties and business of life--a kind of education not to be learned from books, or acquired by any amount of mere literary training. With his usual weight of words Bacon observes, that "Studies teach not their own use; but that is a wisdom without them, and above them, won by observation;" a remark that holds true of actual life, as well as of the cultivation of the intellect itself. For all experience serves to illustrate and enforce the lesson, that a man perfects himself by work more than by reading--that it is life rather than literature, action rather than study, and character rather than biography, which tend perpetually to renovate mankind.

No matter how humble your calling in life may be, take heart from the fact that many of the world's greatest men have had no superior advantages. Lincoln studied law lying on his face before a log-fire; General Garfield drove a mule on a canal tow-path in his boyhood, and George Peabody, owing to the poverty of his family, was an errand boy in a grocery store at the age of eleven.

Great men of science, literature, and art--apostles of great thoughts and lords of the great heart--have belonged to no exclusive class or rank in life. They have come alike, from colleges, workshops, and farm-houses--from the huts of poor men and the mansions of the rich. Some of God's greatest apostles have come from "the ranks." The poorest have sometimes taken the highest places, nor have difficulties apparently the most insuperable proved obstacles in their way. Those very difficulties, in many instances, would even seem to have been their best helpers, by evoking their powers of labor and endurance, and stimulating into life faculties which might otherwise have lain dormant. The instances of obstacles thus surmounted, and of triumphs thus achieved, are indeed so numerous as almost to justify the proverb that "with will one can do anything."

If we took to England, the mother country, a land where the advantages are not nearly so great as in this and the difficulties greater, we shall find noble spirits rising to usefulness and eminence in the face of difficulties equally great.

Shoemakers have given us Sir Cloudesley Shovel the great admiral, Sturgeon the electrician, Samuel Drew the essayist, Gifford the editor of the *Quarterly Review*, Bloomfield the poet, and William Carey the missionary; whilst Morrison, another laborious missionary, was a maker of shoe-lasts. Within the last few years, a profound naturalist has been discovered in the person of a shoemaker at Banff, named

Thomas Edwards, who, while maintaining himself by his trade, has devoted his leisure to the study of natural science in all its brandies, his researches in connection with the smaller crustaceae having been rewarded by the discovery of a new species, to which the name of "Praniza Edwardsii" has been given by naturalists.

Nor have tailors been undistinguished. John Stow, the historian, worked at the trade during some part of his life. Jackson, the painter, made clothes until he reached manhood. The brave Sir John Hawkswood, who so greatly distinguished himself at Poictiers, and was knighted by Edward III for his valor, was in early life apprenticed to a London tailor. Admiral Hobson, who broke the boom at Vigo in 1702, belonged to the same calling. He was working as tailor's apprentice near Bonchurch, in the Isle of Wight, when the news flew through the village that a squadron of men-of-war was sailing off the island. He sprang from the shopboard, and ran down with his comrades to the beach, to gaze upon the glorious sight. The boy was suddenly inflamed with the ambition to be a sailor; and springing into a boat, he rowed off to the squadron, gained the admiral's ship, and was accepted as a volunteer. Years after, he returned to his native village full of honors, and dined off bacon and eggs in the cottage where he had worked as an apprentice.

Oliver Goldsmith was regarded as a dunce in his school days, and Daniel Webster was so dull as a school-boy as not to indicate in any way the great abilities he was to display.

Humbert was a scapegrace when a youth; at sixteen he ran away from home and was by turns servant to a tradesman at Nancy, a workman at Lyons, and a hawker of rabbit-skins. In 1792, he enlisted as a volunteer and in a year he was general of brigade. Kleber, Lefebvre, Suchet, Victor, Lannes, Soult, Massena, St. Cyr, D'Erlon, Murat, Augereau, Bessieres and Ney, all rose from the ranks. In some cases promotion was rapid, in others it was slow. St. Cyr, the son of a tanner of Toul, began life as an actor, after which he enlisted in the chasseurs and was promoted to a captaincy within a year. Victor, Due de Belluno, enlisted in the artillery in 1781: during the events preceding the Revolution he was discharged; but immediately on the outbreak of war he re-enlisted, and in the course of a few months his intrepidity and ability secured his promotion as adjutant-major and chief of battalion. Murat was the son of a village innkeeper in Perigord, where he looked after the horses. He first enlisted in a regiment of chasseurs, from which he was dismissed for insubordination; but again, enlisting he shortly rose to the rank of colonel. Ney enlisted at eighteen in a hussar regiment and gradually advanced step by step; Kleber soon discovered his merits, surnaming him "The Indefatigable," and promoted him to be adjutant-general when only twenty-five.

General Christopher Carson, or "Kit" Carson as he is known to the world, although strictly temperate in his life and as gentle as a blue-eyed child in his manner, ran away from his home in Missouri to the Western wilds, when he was a boy of fourteen. His father wanted him to be a farmer, but Providence had greater if not nobler uses for him. Out in the Rocky Mountains--then a wilderness--he learned the Indian languages, and became as familiar with every trail and pass as the red men.

It was the knowledge gained in those early days that enabled Kit Carson to carry succor to Fremont's men perishing in the mountains. Not only did Carson bring food to the dying men, but when they were strong enough to move he guided them to a place of safety.

This truly great man averted many an Indian war, and did as much for the settlement and civilization of the West as any man of his day-- more, indeed. In the days of secession he was a patriot, and though he might have grown rich at the expense of the Government, he preferred to die a poor and honored man.

Admiral Farragut, although born in East Tennessee, went into the United States Navy at the early age of eleven. He was the youngest midshipman in the service. "Before I had reached the age of sixteen," he says, "I prided myself on my profanity, and could drink with the strongest."

One morning on recovering from a debauch he reviewed the situation and saw the shoals ahead. Then and there he fell on his knees and asked God to help him. From that day on he gave up tobacco, liquor, and profanity, devoted himself to the study of his profession, and so became the greatest Admiral of modern times. "The canal boat captains, when I was a boy," said General Garfield, "were a profane, carousing, ignorant lot, and, as a boy, I was eager to imitate them. But my eyes were opened before I contracted their habits, and I left them."

John B. Gough is an example of such a change of life that should encourage every young man who has made a mis-step.

Among like men of the same class may be ranked the late Richard Cobden, whose start in life was equally humble. The son of a small farmer at Midhurst in Sussex, he was sent at an early age to London and employed as a boy in a warehouse in the City. He was diligent, well-conducted, and eager for information. His master, a man of the old school, warned him against too much reading; but the boy went on in his own course, storing his mind with the wealth found in books. He was promoted from one position of trust to another, became a traveler for his house, secured a large connection, and eventually started in business as a calico-printer at Manchester. Taking an interest in public questions, more especially in popular education, his attention was gradually drawn to the subject of the Corn Laws, to the repeal of which he may be said to have contributed more than all the rest of Parliament.

It would be a mistake, however, to judge from this that all the world's greatest men, started life poor, or that some men of wealth and prominent family have not contributed their share, and have not, by reason of that wealth, sedulously followed a useful life-calling.

Riches are so great a temptation to ease and self-indulgence, to which men are by nature prone, that the glory is all the greater of those who, born to ample fortunes, nevertheless take an active part in the work of their generation--who "scorn delights and live laborious days."

It was a fine thing said of a subaltern officer in the Peninsular campaigns, observed trudging along through mud and mire by the side of his regiment, "There goes 15,000 pounds a year!" and in our own day, the bleak slopes of Sebastopol and the burning soil of India have borne witness to the like noble self-denial and devotion on the part of the richer classes; many a gallant and noble fellow, of rank and estate, having risked his life, or lost it, in one or other of those fields of action, in the service of his country.

Nor have the wealthier classes been undistinguished in the more peaceful pursuits of philosophy and science. Take, for instance, the great names of Bacon, the father of modern philosophy, and of Worcester, Boyle, Cavendish, Talbot and Rosse in science. The last named may be regarded as the great mechanic of the peerage; a man who, if he had not been born a peer, would probably have taken the highest rank as an inventor. So thorough was his knowledge of smith- work that he is said to have been pressed on one occasion to accept the foremanship of a large workshop, by a manufacturer to whom his rank was unknown. The great Rosse telescope, of his own fabrication, is certainly the most extraordinary instrument of the kind that has yet been constructed.

We are apt to think that the wealthy classes in America are addicted to idleness, but, in proportion to their number, they are as usefully industrious as those who are forced to work for a living. The Adams family, of Massachusetts, for more than a century, has been even more distinguished for statesmanship and intellect than for great wealth. The Vanderbilts have all been hard workers and able business men. George Gould seems to be quite as great a financier as his remarkable father. The Astors are distinguished for their literary ability; William Waldorf Astor and his cousin, John Jacob, are authors of great merit. The Lees, of Virginia, have ever been distinguished for energy, intellect, and a capacity for hard work. And so we might cite a hundred examples to prove that even in America, want is not the greatest incentive to effort.

The indefatigable industry of Lord Brougham has become almost proverbial. His public labors extended over a period of upward of sixty years, during which he ranged over many fields--of law, literature, politics, and science--and achieved distinction in them all. How he contrived it, has been to many a mystery. Once, when Sir Samuel Romilly was requested to undertake some new work, he excused himself by saying that he had no time; "but," he added, "go with it to that fellow Brougham, he seems to have time for everything." The secret of it was, that he never left a minute unemployed; withal he possessed a constitution of iron. When arrived at an age at which most men would have retired from the world to enjoy their hard-earned leisure, perhaps to doze away their time in an easy chair, Lord Brougham commenced and prosecuted a series of elaborate investigations as to the laws of Light, and he submitted the results to the most scientific audiences that Paris and London could muster. About the same time, he was passing through the press his admirable sketches of the "Men of Science and Literature of the Reign of George III," and taking his full share of the law business and the political discussions in the House of Lords. Sydney Smith once recommended him to confine himself to only the transaction of so much business as three strong men could get through. But such was Brougham's love of work--long become a habit--that no amount of application seems to have been too great for him; and such was his love of excellence that it has been said of him that if his station in life had been only that of a shoeblack, he would never have rested satisfied until he had become the best shoeblack in England.

CHAPTER XII
SUCCESSFUL FARMING.

Accordng to Holy Writ, man's first calling was agriculture, or, perhaps, horticulture would better express it. Adam was placed in the Garden to till and care for it; and even after he was driven from that blissful abode and compelled to live by the sweat of his brow, he had to go back to the earth from which his body was made to sustain the life breathed into it by Jehovah. But the young men of to-day, and it is much to be regretted, regard farming life with more and more disfavor. To be sure, the greatest fortunes have not been accumulated in farming, but this book will not have accomplished its purpose if it has failed to pint out that lives can be eminently successful without the accumulation of great wealth.

Before proceeding further, let us state a truth which will be convincing to every reader who knows anything at all about the careers of successful men. It is not a little remarkable that the most successful preachers, lawyers, doctors, merchants, and mechanics have had their earliest training on the farm.

As we have before said, the successful life is the one that is happiest and most useful in itself, and which produces happiness and usefulness in others. And as the majority of workers in most civilized lands are directly connected with agriculture, and as all sustenance for our daily lives, and all wealth, save the limited amount that comes from the sea, is directly traceable to the land, it follows that agriculture is the most important of all callings-- and I would say the most honorable, were it not that every calling is honorable that requires for its success energy, industry, intelligence, and honesty.

The United States, above all countries in the world at this time, indeed, above all countries of which history furnishes any record, has been more dependent for

its growth and success on agriculture than on any other vocation. While our manufacturing enterprises rank us next to England among the world's manufacturing
producers, yet more than nine-tenths of our export trade with foreign countries is
in agricultural products, such as: wheat, corn, cotton, tobacco, and beef and pork,
which, under the present system of farming, are as much agricultural productions
as the grain on which the ox and the hog are fattened.

In agriculture, or farming, is included the bulk of the balance of labor not covered by the building and mechanical trades, and the employments growing out of
and connected with them.

Good farming is dependent on good machinery, including tools, and on good
buildings. Doubtless, in its infancy, neither was used, even the hoe and hut being
unknown. Among the first records of producing from the soil, to be found in any
detail, is the raising of corn in Chaldea and Egypt. Sowing seed in the valley of the
Nile, and turning on the swine to tread it into the soil, was one of the methods in
use, and every process of planting and harvesting was of the simplest. As population
grew more dense, and other climates and soils were occupied, better processes were
developed, and more varied were the productions. Animal power and rude tools
were gradually brought into use, and about 1000 years before Christ "a plow with
a beam, share and handles" is mentioned. Then agriculture is spoken of as being in
a flourishing condition, and artificial drainage was resorted to. Grecian farming in
the days of its prosperity attained, in some districts, a creditable advancement, and
the implements in use were, in principle, similar to many of modern construction.
Horses, cattle, swine, sheep, and poultry were bred and continually improved by
importations from other countries. Manuring of the fields was practiced; ground
was often plowed three times before seeding; and sub-soiling and other mixings of
soils were in some cases employed. A great variety of fruit was successfully cultivated, and good farming was a source of pride to the people. The Romans considered it, as Washington did, the most honorable and useful occupation. Each Roman
citizen was allotted a piece of land of from five to fifty acres by the government, and
in after times, when annexations were made, up to five hundred acres were allotted.
The land was generally closely and carefully cultivated, and the most distinguished
citizens considered it their greatest compliment to be called good farmers. The Roman Senate had twenty-eight books, written by a Carthaginian farmer, translated

for the use of the people. The general sentiment among the more intelligent was to hold small farms and till them well; to protect their fields from winds and storms, and to defer building or incurring avoidable expense until fully able.

Thirteen centuries were required to improve upon the plowing of two-thirds of an acre, which in Roman parlance was a *jugarum*, necessitating the labor of two days. The eighteenth century made great improvements in the modes of farming, especially in the matter of tools, machinery, and farm literature; while this century has made marked progress in the raising and harvesting of crops, buildings for farm purposes, and a remarkable improvement in horses, cattle, and other farm stock. Salt was found to be a fertilizer, and vegetation proven to be more beneficial on land in summer than leaving it bare and unoccupied, as had formerly been the theory. Manures were found to be of increased value when mixed, and guanos were introduced.

The Germans and French began improvement in farming before the English, and have well sustained it.

Since the primitive years of the Untied States, her agriculture has attained unparalleled growth, and remains her chief pride and revenue. Those were the years that tried the farmers' souls. They had everything to learn; forests to clear off; seeds and conveniences to secure; roads to open; new grounds to cultivate; buildings to erect, and hostile Indians to watch and fight. South Carolina was the first State to organize an agricultural society, which was accomplished in 1784. Now nearly all the counties of every State have similar organizations, besides those of the States themselves. That they are materially and socially beneficial is unquestioned, barring the effect of horse-racing and its betting accompaniment.

Among the more valuable auxiliaries of the farmer are the agricultural journals of the country, for which hundreds of thousands of dollars are annually expended. With few exceptions they fill the measure of their publication, and the information they furnish, if properly and judiciously used, can have none but a healthy effect. While nine out of every ten farmers doubtless do not do all, nor as well as they know, the benefit and incitement of knowing more can but be beneficial. It is as a bill of fare at an eating-house--while the consumption of every article named therein would be death, the large selection at hand renders possible a wholesome meal.

Mr. Joshua Hill in his work entitled "Thought and Thrift"--which, by the way, would be more valuable if less partisan--has this to say in connection with the business and courage required in agriculture:

"Neglect of aid that may be had in procuring the best results of labor, and inattention in applying it, are faults possessed by many. Every man is by nature possessed of abilities of some sort; and if he has found the right way to use them, he alone is to blame if he does not properly apply them with a view to their highest and best results. There is no use for a rule if there be no measures to take; thee is no use for a reason if men do not heed it. Human experiences are full of wise counsel for those who desire to learn and do so; but for those who close their eyes and wait for results without effort, the records containing them would just as well never have been written. There is an absolutely fixed law of nature that denies to man anything that he does not receive from some kind of labor, except to such as live by favor and robbery, and not by work. There are many examples of those who are said to 'live by their wits,' but the problem as to how it is done may never be solved. Nor does it need to be solved, as no man should justly expect to enjoy anything which has not been procured by his own labor. Those who most appreciated the comforts of life are those who create them for themselves. In knowing how what we have is obtained, lies its chief value to us. Men naturally take pride in the possession of a treasure in proportion to the trouble involved in securing it. Whoever would thrive in his farming must bend his whole will and purpose to it. Nothing which can be done to-day should be put off till to-morrow. To-morrow may never come, and should it come, may not changed conditions and difficulties render set tasks impossible? Under some circumstances men trust to fortune, without serious errors, in postponing the execution of appointed tasks. The maxim that 'procrastination is the thief of time' points a moral implied in itself, and is unquestionably true in a majority of instances. Men of business are often careful in some matters, to the neglect of others more important. Different men have different methods of business, which, considering differences of constitution and manner of application, is only natural; not dangerous, but rather beneficial. No two men go to work in the same way, notwithstanding they may have both learned of the same teacher, or been instructed upon the same principle. The greater trouble lies in improper application and inattention to details. Trifles make up the sum of life, as cents make dollars. An overanxious man, he who makes great haste to be rich, seldom prospers long in any undertaking. Possibilities, not probabilities, should be the guide. A sanguine disposition may or may not be useful in business. Disappointment often follows sanguine hopes. A good business man calculates closely; does not allow anticipation to run away with his judgment, nor imagine that any good result can follow a false move.

"For these reasons, the farmer needs to think and to reason more; to attend more strictly to business rules and methods, and to exercise a greater courage and persistency in applying them. 'Work while it is day,' says the Scriptures, 'for the night cometh when no man can work.' Command the present moment that shakes gold from its wings. That the future may bring bread for his family, the farmer sows seed in confidence, and awaits the harvest in hope. But if he fails to do what is necessary to a proper yield from his crop, he has made a failure of the talents committed to him. Men must acknowledge the responsibility that rest upon them, and meet it with that true courage which directs them aright. The lack of knowledge does not imply lack of ability to think and to reason. All men, unless of idiotic, impaired, or diseased minds, are possessed of the faculty of reason, and should use it for the purpose for which it was given-- to supply needed helps to our temporal existence. From thought comes ability, and from ability system, courage, attention, application, the most valuable aids to every man of business.

"But in farming as in every other calling the first great requisite is self-reliance. The man who depends upon his neighbors, as Aesop illustrates in one of his fables, never has his work done. But when he says that he will do it himself on a certain day, then it is prudent for the bird that has been nesting in his grainfield to change her habitation."

CHAPTER XIII
AS TO PUBLIC LIFE.

The relations of the citizen to the state, and of the state to the citizen, are reciprocal. Every man who becomes a member of an established government, whether it be voluntary, as where an oath of allegiance is taken to obey the laws, or involuntary, as by birth, which is the case of a majority of all citizens, he surrenders certain natural rights in consideration of the protection which the government throws about him.

In a state of nature, man is free to do as he pleases, without any recognition of the rights of others; and his power to have his own way is entirely dependent on the physical strength and courage which he has to enforce it. This is why, in a savage state, war is the almost constant business of the men, and the strongest and the bravest of the lawless mob, tribe, or clan usually becomes leader.

When through either of these agencies a man finds himself a member of an established government, he owes to that government implicit obedience to its laws, in consideration of the protection to life and property which that government throws about him.

In consideration of the protection which the banded many, known as the state, gives to the individual, the individual pledges implicit obedience to the laws of the state.

Horace says : *Dulci et decorum est pro patria mori*--meaning that it is brave and right to die for one's country. Old Dr. Sam Johnson, like his successor, Carlyle, was apt to sneer at the grander impulses of humanity. He said on one occasion: "Patriotism is the last resort of a scoundrel." And yet we know that the noblest characters of all history have been the men who felt, with Horace, that it was noble to die for one's country.

Americans, perhaps more than any other people in the world at this time, have an intense appreciation of this spirit of patriotism. From the days of the Revolution to the present time, our most prominent and most respected characters have been the men who, in the forum or in the field, have devoted their lives to the preservation and elevation of the Republic.

Public life has its rewards, but they rarely come to the honest man in the form of dollars. Franklin, Jackson, Taylor, Jolinson, Grant, Garfield, and Lincoln were all the sons of poor men, and they died poor themselves; but who can say that their lives were not grandly successful.

An interest in politics should be the duty of everyone, but the young man who enters public life for the sake of the money he may accumulate from office, starts out as a traitor to his country and an ingrate to his fellows.

Public life should be an unselfish life. The service of the public requires the strongest bodies, the clearest brains, and the purest hearts, and the man who devotes his life to this great purpose must find his reward in a duty well performed, rather than in the financial emoluments of office.

Duty is the spirit of patriotism, and while this spirit should run through every act in every calling, it must particularly distinguish the man who has entered the public service as a soldier or civil official. It is duty that leads the soldier to face hardships and death without flinching, and the same high impulse should stimulate the conduct where there is no physical danger.

Samuel Smiles, to whom we are indebted for much that is valuable in this work, has the following to say in this connection about duty:

"Duty is a thing that is due, and must be paid by every man who would avoid present discredit and eventual moral insolvency. It is an obligation--a debt--which can only be discharged by voluntary effort and resolute action in the affairs of life.

"Duty embraces man's whole existence. It begins in the home, where there is the duty which children owe to their parents on the one- hand, and the duty which parents owe to their children on the other. There are, in like manner, the respective duties of husbands and wives, of masters and servants; while outside the home there are the duties which men and women owe to each other as friends and neighbors, as employers and employed, as governors and governed.

"'Render, therefore,' says St. Paul, 'to all their dues: tribute to whom tribute is due; custom to whom custom; fear to whom fear; honor to whom honor. Owe no man anything, but to love one another; for he that loveth another hath fulfilled the law.'

"Thus duty rounds the whole of life, from our entrance into it until our exit from it--duty to superiors, duty to inferiors, and duty to equals--duty to man, and duty to God. Wherever there is power to use or to direct, there is duty. For we are but as stewards, appointed to employ the means entrusted to us for our own and for others' good.

"The abiding sense of duty is the very crown of character. It is the upholding law of man in his highest attitudes. Without it, the individual totters and falls before the first puff of adversity or temptation; whereas, inspired by it, the weakest becomes strong and full of courage. 'Duty,' says Mrs. Jameson, 'is the cement which binds the whole moral edifice together; without which, all power, goodness, intellect, truth, happiness, love itself, can have no permanence; but all the fabric of existence crumbles away from under us, and leaves us at last sitting in the midst of a ruin, astonished at our own desolation.'

"Duty is based upon a sense of justice--justice inspired by love, which is the most perfect form of goodness. Duty is not a sentiment, but a principle pervading the life: and it exhibits itself in conduct and in acts, which are mainly determined by man's conscience and free will."

Sir John Packington, one of England's most famous men, said in speaking of his public life:

"I am indebted for whatever measure of success I have attained in my public life, to a combination of moderate abilities with honesty of intention, firmness of purpose, and steadiness of conduct. If I were to offer advice to any young man anxious to make himself useful in public life, I would sum up the results of my experience in three short rules--rules so simple that any man may act upon them. My first rule will be, leave it to others to judge of what duties you are capable, and for what position you are fitted; but never refuse to give your services in whatever capacity it my be the opinion of others who are competent to judge that you may benefit your neighbors and your country. My second rule is, when you agree to undertake public duties, concentrate every energy and faculty in your possession with the determination to discharge those duties to the best of your ability. Lastly, I would counsel you that, in deciding on the line which you will take in public affairs, you should be guided in your decision by that which, after mature deliberation, you believe to be right, and not by that which, in the passing hour, may happen to be fashionable or popular."

Another author equally eminent writes in the same vein:

"The first great duty of every citizen is that of an abiding love for his country. This is one of the native instincts of the noble heart. History tells of many a devoted hero, reared under an oppressive despotism, and groaning under unjust exactions, with little in the character of his ruler to excite anything like generous enthusiasm, who yet has shed his blood and given up his treasures in willing sacrifice for his country's good. In a country such as this we live in, it is the duty of every man to be a patriot, and to love and serve it with an affection that is commensurate both with the priceless cost of her liberties, and the greatness of her civil and religious privileges. Indeed, however it may be in other lands, in this one the youth may be said to draw in the love of country with his native air; and it is justly taken for granted that all will seek and maintain her interests, as that the child shall love its mother, on whose bosom it has been cradled, and of whose life it is a part.

"In no other country more than this is it important that all should rightly understand and faithfully fulfill the duties of citizenship. While ignorance is the natural stronghold of tyranny, knowledge is the very throne of civil liberty. It is the interest of despotism to foster a blind, unreasoning obedience to arbitrary law; but where, as with us, almost the humblest has a voice in the administration of public affairs, more depends upon the enlightened sentiments of the masses than upon even the skill of temporary rulers, or the character of existing laws."

A generation ago, when the integrity of the Union was threatened, the rich and the poor, the young and the old, particularly in what were known as the Free States, gave up all for the defense of the Republic. It should be said, in justice to those who fought on the opposite side, that no matter how much mistaken, they were in their own hearts as honest, and by their heroic sacrifices proved themselves to be as brave and unselfish, as the gallant men who won in the appeal to arms.

If to-day the honor or the integrity of the Republic were assailed, every man capable of bearing arms, irrespective of the past differences of themselves or their fathers, would answer the country's call in teeming millions, and prove the truth of the Latin poet's adage, that it is right and noble to die for ones country.

A manly people should cultivate a manly spirit, and be prepared, if need be, to defend their rights by force, but in the better day, whose light is coming, we believe that nobler and more equitable means of adjusting internal and international differences can be found than by an appeal to arms.

Believing then that every young man who is worthy his American citizenship would willingly risk his life in defense of his nation's flag--which, after all, is simply the emblem of what his nation stands for--he should be willing, if duty requires it, to serve his country with equal fidelity in times of peace.

It is to be regretted that men of the stamp of those who gave their lives or risked them and have poured out their wealth with unstinted hand when the life of the Republic was in danger, should, in days of peace, regard "politics"--which means an interest in public affairs-- with something like contempt.

It may be argued that politics has fallen into the hands of a rough and unprincipled class, who make it a profession for the sake of the gain it offers. To a certain extent this is true; but the men who are responsible for this state of affairs are not the professional politicians, but the good citizens, who are in the majority, and who could control, if they would, but who unpatriotically neglect their duty to the public, or ignore it in the presence of their individual interests. One of the best signs of the times is the fact that civil service has come into our politics to stay. Through this service, the young aspirant for office, irrespective of his politics, stands an examination before impartial commissioners, and is rated according to his qualifications. Once he enters the public service, he cannot be discharged except for incapacity, and this must be proven before a proper tribunal. The rewards of public office, excepting in a few cases where the positions depend upon the votes of the people, are never great. And, unfortunately, under our system the aspirant for an elective office usually spends as much as the office will pay him during his term, if he depends upon its honest emoluments. But to the young man who is not ambitious and who will live contentedly a life of routine with a limited compensation, a public life has many advantages. The salary continues, irrespective of the weather or seasons, and there is connected with the place a certain respect. No matter how humble the position of a man in the public service, a certain dignity must always attach to him who is at once a servant and a representative of the people.

CHAPTER XIV
THE NEED OF CONSTANT EFFORT.

It matters not what talent or genius a man may possess, no natural gift can compensate for hard, persistent toil. The Romans had a maxim as true to-day as it was when first uttered: "*Labor omnia vincit*," Toil conquers all things. The earliest Christians lived in communities and had all things in common. One of their precepts-- a precept up to which all lived--was: "*Laborare est orare*," To work is to pray.

Someone has said that the difference between the genius and the ordinary man is that the genius has a tireless capacity for patient, hard work, while the other regards effort as a painful exaction, and is ever looking forward to the time when he can rest.

It is encouraging to know that the world's hardest workers have lived the longest lives. In this alone, labor is its own reward; but enduring success never came to a poor man without an unflagging patience and an unceasing toil.

Honorable industry, says one, travels the same road with duty; and Providence has closely linked both with happiness. The gods, says the poet, have placed labor and toil on the way leading to the Elysian fields. Certain it is that no bread eaten by man is so sweet as that earned by his own labor, whether bodily or mental. By labor the earth has been subdued, and man redeemed from barbarism; nor has a single step in civilization been made without it. Labor is not only a necessity and a duty, but a blessing; only the idler feels it to be a curse. The duty of work is written on the thews and muscles of the limbs, the mechanism of the hand, the nerves and lobes of the brain--the sum of whose healthy action is satisfaction and enjoyment. In the school of labor is taught the best practical wisdom; nor is a life of manual employment, as we shall hereafter find, incompatible with high mental culture.

Hugh Miller, than whom none knew better the strength and the weakness belonging to the lot of labor, stated the result of his experience to be, that work, even the hardest, is full of pleasure and materials for self-improvement. He held honest labor to be the best of teachers, and that the school of toil is the nobles of schools--save only the Christian one; that it is a school in which the ability of being useful is imparted, the spirit of independence learned, and the habit of persevering effort acquired. He was even of opinion that the training of the mechanic--by exercise which it gives to his observant faculties, from his daily dealing with things actual and practical, and the close experience of life which he acquires--better fits a man for picking his way along the journey of life, and is more favorable to his growth as a man, emphatically speaking, than the training afforded by any other condition.

Watt, the inventor of the steam engine, was one of the most industrious of men; and the story of his life proves, what all experience confirms, that it is not the man of the greatest natural vigor and capacity who achieves the highest results, but he who employs his powers with the greatest industry and the most carefully disciplined skill--the skill that comes by labor, application, and experience. Many men in his time knew far more than Watt, but none labored so assiduously as he did to turn all that he did know to useful practical purposes. He was, above all things, most persevering in the pursuit of facts. He cultivated carefully that habit of active attention on which all the higher working qualities of the mind mainly depend. Indeed, Mr. Edgeworth entertained the opinion that the difference of intellect in men depends more upon the early cultivation of this *habit of attention*, than upon any great disparity between the powers of one individual and another.

Arkwright, one of the world's greatest mechanics, and the inventor of the spinning jenny, was famed for his unceasing industry.

Like most of our great mechanicians, he sprang from the ranks. He was born in Preston in 1732. His parents were very poor, and he was the youngest of thirteen children. He was never at school; the only education he received he gave to himself; and to the last he was only able to write with difficulty. When a boy, he was apprenticed to a barber, and after learning the business, he set up for himself in Bolton, where he occupied an underground cellar, over which he put up the sign, "come to the subterraneous barber--he shaves for a penny." The other barbers found their customers leaving them, and reduced their prices to his standard, when

Arkwright, determined to push his trade, announced his determination to give "A clean shave for a half- penny."

At the close of his life, John Jacob Astor was the wealthiest man in the United States, and the immense fortune he left has been largely increased through his wise investments and the habits of business which he seems to have transmitted with his fortune to his descendants.

His life is a most interesting one, particularly to the young man who stands facing the world without friends or fortune to aid him. But young Astor had one quality to start with, a quality which success never lessened, and that was the capacity for unceasing industry.

He was born of peasant parents in the village of Waldorf, near the great university town of Heidelberg in Germany. When sixteen years of age he was crowded out of the hive by increasing brothers and sisters, and without education or experience, he started out to make his way in the world.

In the days of his great prosperity, he used to tell, with delight mingled with sadness, of the day when he left father, and mother, and home, which he was never to see together again. He used to say: "I had only two dollars in my pocket, and all my clothes were tied up in a handkerchief fastened at the end of a stick. When I had climbed the high hill above the village, I sat down to rest my heart rather than my feet, and to look back at the loved scenes of my childhood. Before leaving home it was decided that I should make my way to London--then the city of promise to many young Germans. While I sat there, I made three resolutions, which during my life I have never broken. I had never gambled, but I had known others to do so, and my first resolve was not to follow their example. The second resolution was to be strictly honest in all my dealings, and this I have tried to adhere to. The third resolution was quite as important as the other two together; it was that so long as God gave me health and strength I should be unceasingly industrious."

John Jacob Astor, as a man, faithfully carried out the resolutions he made as a boy, and the world knows the consequences.

When the impartial historian comes to write the life of Horace Greeley, no matter how much he may object to his policies and politics, he will give him credit for honesty, courage, perseverance, and an industry that knew no fatigue.

While barely in his teens, young Greeley, whose father was making a desperate effort to support a large family on a poor farm in New Hampshire, started in to work for himself. His early education consisted of a few winter terms in a common school. Before he was seventeen he had learned the printer's trade, and then resolved not only to support himself, but to help his parents. Realizing his want of education, he devoted every minute he could spare from work or sleep to study.

Speaking of these early days, Mr. Greeley said:

"There was many a heavy load placed on my shoulders, but I staggered on and bore it as best I could. Many an uncongenial task was forced upon me, but I can honestly say I never shirked it. If I have succeeded in my chosen profession, it has not been due to my early advantages, for I had none, but to my strong belief that patient industry would triumph in the end."

When Horace Greeley was twenty years of age he was working in a printing office in Erie, Pennsylvania, and determined to better his fortunes by coming to New York. He had saved up one hundred and twenty dollars, and of this he sent one hundred to his father, and with the rest he turned his face to the great city, about six hundred miles away. He traveled the entire distance on foot, and reached New York with fifteen dollars, the whole trip having cost him but five.

Poorly clad, tall, gawky, and green-looking, he entered the city where he had neither friend nor acquaintance. For weeks he tramped the streets, looking vainly for work, his cash gradually growing less, but his spirits never failing. At length he found employment at his trade, where his integrity and unceasing industry soon made him conspicuous. Step by step, he worked his way up, never forgetting the poor family in Vermont, till at length he was able to establish the *New York Tribune*, which survives as a monument of his perseverance and industry. Although his early training was so defective, he gave every spare minute to study, and with such success that he became not only a great leader, but one of the most perfect masters of the English language. His name will long live after many writers and statesmen of greater pretensions are forgotten.

As an example of what perseverance, fortitude and energy will do, Horace Greeley's story of his own life should be studied by every ambitious young man.

Horace Greelev never laid claim to physical courage, but he had that higher courage and industry without which enduring success is impossible. In speaking of this admirable quality, a famous author says:

"The greater part of the courage that is needed in the world is not of an heroic kind. Courage may be displayed in everyday life as well as on historic fields of action. There needs, for example, the common courage to be honest--the courage to resist temptation--the courage to speak the truth--the courage to be what we really are, and not to pretend to be what we are not--the courage to live honestly within our own means, and not dishonestly upon the means of others.

"A great deal of the unhappiness, and much of the vice, of the world is owing to weakness and indecision of purpose--in other words, to lack of courage and want of industry. Men may know what is right, and yet fail to exercise the courage to do it; they may understand the duty they have to do, but will not summon up the requisite resolution to perform it. The weak and undisciplined man is at the mercy of every temptation; he cannot say no,' but falls before it. And if his companionship be bad, he will be all the easier led away by bad example into wrong-doing.

"Nothing can be more certain than that the character can only be sustained and strengthened by its own energetic action. The will, which is the central force of character, must be trained to habits of decision--otherwise it will neither be able to resist evil nor to follow good. Decision gives the power of standing firmly, when to yield, however slightly, might be only the first step in a downhill course to ruin.

"Calling upon others for help in forming a decision is worse than useless. A man must so train his habits as to rely upon his own powers and depend upon his own courage in moments of emergency. Plutarch tells of a king of Macedon who, in the midst of an action, withdrew into the adjoining town under pretence of sacrificing to Hercules; whilst his opponent Emilius, at the same time that he implored the Divine aid, sought for victory sword in hand, and won the battle. And so it ever is in the actions of daily life.

"Many are the valiant purposes formed, that end merely in words; deeds intended, that are never done; designs projected, that are never begun; and all for want of a little courageous decision. Better far the silent tongue but the eloquent deed. For in life, and in business, dispatch is better than discourse; and the shortest of all is *Doing*. 'In matters of great concern, and which must be done,' says Tillotson, 'there is no surer argument of a weak mind than irresolution--to be undetermined when the case is so plain and the necessity so urgent. To be always intending to live a new life, but never to find time to set about it--this is as if a man should put off eating and drinking and sleeping from one day to another, until he is starved and destroyed.'"

CHAPTER XV
SOME OF LABOR'S COMPENSATIONS.

Although it is better for every young man, if possible, to adhere to one thing, yet, as we shall see when we come to treat of the life of that remarkable man Peter Cooper, change does not necessarily mean vacillation. For the mere sake of consistency a man would be foolish who neglected a good chance to succeed in another field. Edison started life as a newsboy, but it would be folly to say that he should have stuck to that very respectable, but not usually lucrative occupation. Morse, the inventor of the telegraph, was an artist till middle life. Alexander T. Stewart and James Gordon Bennett, the one a most successful journalist, and the other the greatest merchant of his day, began life as school-teachers. And so we might continue the list; but even these examples do not warrant the belief that a change of calling is necessary to success, but rather that the change may increase the chances. As a rule, however, the changes have been forced by unforeseen circumstances, of which these strong men were quick to see the advantages.

In beginning the life journey, as in starting out on a day's journey, it is of great importance to have a destination in view. In every effort there should be kept in mind the end to be attained--an ideal to achieve which every faculty must be enlisted.

Men whose lives have been eminently successful tell us that their greatest reward was not found in the accomplishment of their life purpose, but in the slow, but certain advance made from day to day.

The joy of travel does not lie in reaching the destination, but in the companions met with on the journey, the changing scenery through which the traveler passes, and even the inconveniences that break up the monotony of the ordinary routine life. It is so with our life- work. The cradle and the grave mark the beginning and the end of the journey, but the joy of living lies in the varied incident and effort to be met with between the two.

It is well for us that this is so; well for us that we do not have to wait for the reward till the end comes.

We may, as in the cases named, change our means of travel, but so long as success is our purpose, it matters not so much what variation we may make in the route, when we seek to attain it.

The old-fashioned country school debating societies had one subject that never lost its popularity, and on which the rural orators exhausted their eloquence and ingenuity: "Resolved, that there is more happiness in participation than in antici-pation." We doubt if any debating society ever settled the question, in a way that would be acceptable to all. As a rule the younger people decided, irrespective of the argument, that participation was the most desirable; but the older people wisely shook their heads and took the other side of the case.

Often when the end has been gained, it has been discovered that the reward was not worth the effort, and that the full compensation was gained in the peace, the regular habits, the health, and the sense of duty well-performed which kept up the hope and the strength during the long years of toil.

There is a temperance in eating, as well as in drinking; even honest labor when carried to an excess that impairs the powers of mind and body, may be classed with intemperance; indeed, it should be a part of every young man's course of self-study to learn his own physical and mental limitations.

There is everything in knowing how to work, and in learning when to rest. One of the rewards of judicious labor, and by no means the least of them is--health. Health is not only essential to the happiness of ourselves and of those with whom we come into contact, but no permanent success can be won without it.

Benjamin Franklin, himself a model of industry and of good health, even in old age, says:

"I have always worked hard, but I have regarded as sinful the haste and toil that sap the health. There is reason why disease should seize on the idler, but the indus-trious man, whose toil is well- regulated, should have no occasion for a physician, unless in case of accident. Labor, like virtue, is its own reward."

In looking over the callings of people who have retained all their powers to an age so long beyond the allotted time as to seem phenomenal, there is not one case that we can recall where the life has not been distinguished for temperance, orderliness, and persistent but temperate industry.

The health that waits upon labor is among its best results, as it must continue to be among its greatest blessings. More particularly is health to be derived from out-door employment, as life on the farm and an active participation in its many and varied labors. Physical exercise is essential to health, under any and all circumstances, whether it be in the nature of labor or recreation. It must be borne in mind, however, that in labor are to be found the surest correctives of many abuses of health, as bringing into play influences of the more satisfactory sort upon the mind as considered in contrast to idleness. Idleness is the parent of many vices, some one says, and it is true. The freedom from the annoying reflection that one is making no use of physical or mental abilities to secure protection from want and suffering, sweetens labor and gives it a value which all true men must appreciate and carefully consider. How often have the wearied journalist and accountant, tired out in body and mind at the desk of unremitting application, found, in the life and labor of the farm and shop, relief and a return to the blessings of health. There are other occupations and employments just as necessary, but many of them are pursued under considerations not leading to, but rather away from, health. Any one, however, may take from business enough time for rest and healthful exercise. It is in purifying and driving away from man the tendencies to evil that, in idleness, prey too continually and strongly upon him, and which he cannot long successfully resist, that labor possesses its greatest benefit. The atmosphere of diligent labor usefully directed is always of a healthy nature. Into it cannot enter the many foes that assail the idle, who have not the shield of protection that labor gives to all who enter its hallowed gateway. Labor dignifies and ennobles when in moderation; it permits the enjoyment of comforts and luxuries, and gives to home its sacred charm; it dashes away the bitter cup of poverty, and gives instead the nourishing and acceptable food of contentment; it dispels dread conceits of coming evil, and dries the tears of the afflicted. Labor is man's heaven-born heritage in exchange for the curse of disobedience, and yet men are ungrateful and disposed to quarrel with their truest friends. What truer and better friend can anyone possess than useful labor, the key that unlocks the casket of wisdom and exposes to our startled gaze the treasures that lie within? For every honest and determined end of labor there is sure reward. "There is no reward without toil" is a proverb as old as history and as true to-day as when it first found lodgment in the minds and hearts of men. The faithful servant of labor hears in every blow he strikes the sure sound of the power committed to him and which will bring him the fine gold of merited approval.

The health in labor, considered in all of the relations attaching to it, further brings a comfort and satisfaction which cannot be too highly estimated. The surest remedy that can be applied, when men are suffering from defeat in business and the attendant consequences, is renewed and persistent labor. Who can measure the value of labor? It is a possession that cannot be stolen, and only ceases to serve when men, from exhausted energies or enfeebled age, can no longer command it. From the beginning to the end of life it waits upon us, and whoever will use it will not be deprived of its wonderful and magnificent bounties.

As labor is man's greatest blessing, so is indolence his greatest curse. As labor is health, so indolence is disease. Man in a condition of idleness is about as useless a thing as is to be found in nature. He prefers to live by some one else's labor. The world owes him a living and he manages somehow to get it. But he is an industrious collector, although he would walk a mile to get around work. He attaches himself, like the mistletoe, to whoever will support him. He is a true parasite. His tongue has but little end to it. It wags from morning to night; invents seemingly plausible theories of work, but never attempts them. He is full of advice to all who will listen. Can such a man be healthy? He *cannot* enjoy good health because he is too lazy to do so. No way has as yet been found to make him healthy and put him to work. He cannot be got rid of. People who labor and who are compelled to help this poor creature do not make much effort to turn him in the direction of labor. They are too busy to take any account of him; so he is left to his misery and poverty. He has not a grain of independence in his whole composition. He pines and dies at last, and the world is better for his being out of it. But like mushrooms, these people spring up. Many infest our large cities, and these are dignified by the city directories as "floating population." The term is very nearly correct; they float for a time upon the current, until borne away to another port where there is better and safer anchorage. Where free lunches are abundant there the idler may be found. For this privilege he is sometimes obliged to do a little work. But how it grieves him! His whole aim is to get drink, a little food, and less clothing. He of course, uses tobacco; but this he must obtain in some way that does not call for money, for of that he has none and never can have, unless he go to work--and this is highly improbable. He has got to that point that he cannot work. He is too unhealthy and his influence is corrupting. Nobody will give him employment, so he must keep on to the end of the chapter. An even more disgusting specimen is the idler who develops into a sneakthief and the more genteel sort of gentry-- gamblers and workers of chances. These are, perhaps, to be included in the list of those who live by their wits and not by any kind of labor.

If there is any worse disease than idleness, it has not yet been discovered. Good and true men, who value the rewards of labor, look upon idleness with a dread that equals that of yellow fever; for it is more general in its effects and more to be detested. While there may sometimes be luck in leisure, indolence never pays.

But the effects of persistent, systematic effort are not confined to ourselves; the example is contagious and acts as a guide and a stimulus to others in the life battle. The good done and the help given to friends in this way are incalculable, and are not the least of the rewards labor bestows before the end is attained.

Dr. Miller in his able work "The Building of Character," says very aptly in this connection:

"We all need human friendship. We need it especially in our times of darkness. He does not well, he lives not wisely, who in the days of prosperity neglects to gather about his life a few loving friends, who will be a strength to him in the days of stress and need."

There is a time to show sympathy, when it is golden; when this time has passed, and we have only slept meanwhile, we may as well sleep on. You did not go near your friend when he was fighting his battle alone. You might have helped him then. What use is there in your coming to him now, when he has conquered without your aid? You paid no attention to your neighbor when he was bending under life's loads, and struggling with difficulties, obstacles, and adversities. You let him alone then. You never told him that you sympathized with him. You never said a brave, strong word of cheer to him in those days. You never even scattered a handful of flowers on his hard path. Now that he is dead and lying in his coffin, what is the use in your standing beside his still form, and telling the people how nobly he battled, how heroically he lived; and speaking words of commendation? No, no; having let him go on, unhelped, uncheered, unencouraged, through the days when he needed so sorely your warm sympathy, and craved so hungrily your cheer, you may as well sleep on and take your rest, letting him alone unto the end. Nothing can be done now. Too laggard are the feet that come with comfort when the time for comfort is past.

"Ah! woe for the word that is never said   Till the ear is deaf to hear; And woe for the lack to the fainting head   Of the ringing shout of cheer; Ah! woe for the laggard feet that tread   In the mournful wake of the bier. A pitiful thing the gift to-day   That is dross and nothing worth, Though if it had come but yesterday,   It had brimmed with sweet the earth; A fading rose in a death-cold hand,   That perished in want and dearth."

Shall we not take our lesson from the legend of the robin that plucked a thorn from the Savior's brow, and thus sought to lessen his pain, rather than from the story of the disciples, who slept and failed to give the help which the Lord sought from their love? Thus can we strengthen those whose burdens are heavy, and whose struggles and sorrows are sore.

All noble effort, as Sarah K. Bolton beautifully expresses it, is its own reward:

"I like the man who faces what he must With step triumphant and a heart of cheer; Who fights the daily battle without fear; Sees his hopes fail, yet keeps unfaltering trust That God is God; that, somehow, true and just, His plans work out for mortals; not a tear Is shed when fortune, which the world holds dear, Falls from his grasp. Better, with love, a crust, Than living in dishonor; envies not Nor loses faith in man; but does his best, Nor ever murmurs at his humbler lot; But with a smile and words of hope, gives zest To every toiler. He alone is great Who, by a life heroic, conquers fate."

"After I have completed an invention," says Thomas A. Edison, "I seem to lose interest in it. One might think that the money value of an invention constituted its reward to the man who loves his work. But, speaking for myself, I can honestly say this is not so. Life was never so full of joy to me, as when a poor boy I began to think out improvements in telegraphy, and to experiment with the cheapest and crudest appliances. But, now that I have all the appliances I need, and am my own master, I continue to find my greatest pleasure, and so my reward, in the work that precedes what the world calls success."

Mr. Gladstone, the great English statesman, and though nearing four score and ten, still one of the most industrious of men, says:

"I have found my greatest happiness in labor. I early formed the habit of industry, and it has been its own reward. The young are apt to think that rest means a cessation from all effort, but I have found the most perfect rest in changing effort. If brain-weary over books and study, go out into the blessed sunlight and the pure air, and give heartfelt exercise to the body. The brain will soon become calm and rested. The efforts of nature are ceaseless. Even in our sleep, the heart throbs on. If these great forces ceased for an instant death would follow. I try to live close to nature, and to imitate her in my labors. The compensation is sound sleep, a wholesome digestion, and powers that are kept at their best; and this I take it is the chief reward of industry."

"If I ever get time from work," said Horace Greeley one day, "I'll go a-fishing, for I was fond of it when a boy." But he never went a-fishing, never indulged in a healthful change of exercise, and the result was a mind thrown out of balance, and death in the prime of life. We all need a restful change at times.

CHAPTER XVI
PATIENCE AND PERSEVERANCE.

If great success were possible only to men of great talents, then there would be but little success in the world.

It has been said that talent is quite as much the ability to stick to a thing, as the aptitude to do it better than another. "I will fight it out on this line, if it takes all summer." This statement of General Grant does not indicate the man of genius, but it does show the man of indomitable perseverance, a perseverance to which he owed all his success, for it is well known that he was a very modest, and by no means a brilliant man. The key to his character was pertinacity: the secret of his success was perseverance.

"I will to-day thrash the Mexicans, or die a-trying!" was what Sam Houston said to an aide, the morning of the battle of San Jacinto. And he won.

The soldier who begins the battle in doubt is half beaten in advance.

The man who loses heart after one failure is a fool to make a beginning.

There is a great deal in good preparation, but there is a great deal more in heroic perseverance. The man who declines to make a beginning till everything he thinks he may need is ready for his hand, is very apt to make a failure. The greatest things have been achieved by the simplest means. It is the ceaseless chopping that wears away the stone. The plodder may be laughed at, and the brilliant man who accomplishes great things at a leap admired; but we all remember the fable of the tortoise and the hare; the latter, confident of her powers, stopped to rest; the former, aware of his limitations, persevered and toiled laboriously on--and he won the race.

We do not wish to be understood as underestimating genius. We believe in it; but one of its strongest characteristics is perseverance, and the next is its capacity to accomplish great results with the simplest means.

"Easy come, easy go." Those things that are acquired without much effort, are usually appreciated according to the effort expended. Determination has a strong *will*; stubbornness has a strong *won't*. The one is characterized by perseverance, and it builds up; the other, having no purpose but blind self, ends in destruction.

It is a fact at once remarkable and encouraging that no man of great genius who has left his mark on his times, ever believed that his success was due to gifts that lifted him above his fellows. The means by which he rose were within the reach of all, and perseverance was a prime requisite.

The greatest results in life are usually attained by simple means, and the exercise of ordinary qualities. The common life of everyday, with its cares, necessities, and duties, affords ample opportunity for acquiring experience of the best kind; and its most beaten paths provide the true worker with abundant scope for effort and room for self-improvement. The road of human welfare lies along the old highway of steadfast well-doing; and they who are the most persistent, and work in the truest spirit, will usually be the most successful.

Fortune has often been blamed for her blindness; but fortune is not so blind as men are. Those who look into practical life will find that fortune is usually on the side of the industrious, as the winds and waves are on the side of the best navigators. In the pursuit of even the highest branches of human inquiry, the commoner qualities are found the most useful--such as common sense, attention, application, and perseverance. Genius may not be necessary, though even genius of the highest sort does not disdain the use of these ordinary qualities. The very greatest men have been among the least believers in the power of genius, and as worldly wise and persevering as successful men of the commoner sort. Some have even defined genius to be only common sense intensified. A distinguished teacher and president of a college spoke of it as the power of making efforts. John Foster held it to be the power of lighting one's own fire. Buffon said of genius, "It is patience."

Newton's was unquestionably a mind of the very highest order, and yet, when asked by what means he had worked out his extraordinary discoveries, he modestly answered, "By always thinking unto them." At another time he thus expressed his method of study: "I keep the subject continually before me, and wait till the first dawnings open slowly by little and little into a full and clear light." It was in Newton's case as in every other, only by diligent application and perseverance that his great reputation was achieved. Even his recreation consisted in change of study, laying down one subject to take up another. To Dr. Bentley he said: "If I have done the public any service, it is due to nothing but industry and patient thought." So Kepler, another great philosopher, speaking of his studies and his progress, said: "As in Virgil, 'Fama mobilitate viget, vires acquirit eundo,' so it was with me, that the diligent thought on these things was the occasion of still further thinking; until at last I brooded with the whole energy of my mind upon the subject."

The extraordinary results effected by dint of sheer industry and perseverance, have led many distinguished men to doubt whether the gift of genius be so exceptional an endowment as it is usually supposed to be. Thus Voltaire held that it is only a very slight line of separation that divides the man of genius from the man of ordinary mould. Beccaria was even of opinion that all men might be poets and orators, and Reynolds that they might be painters and sculptors. If this were really so, that stolid Englishman might not have been so very far wrong after all, who, on Canova's death, inquired of his brother whether it was "his intention to carry on the business!" Locke, Helvetuis, and Diderot believed that all men have an equal aptitude for genius, and that what some are able to effect, under the laws which regulate the operations of the intellect, must also be within the reach of others who, under like circumstances, apply themselves to like pursuits. But while admitting to the fullest extent the wonderful achievements of labor, and recognizing the fact that men of the most distinguished genius have invariably been found the most indefatigable workers, it must nevertheless be sufficiently obvious that, without the original endowment of heart and brain, no amount of labor, however well applied, could have produced a Shakespeare, a Newton, a Beethoven, or a Michael Angelo.

Dalton, the chemist, repudiated the notion of his being a "genius" attributing everything which he had accomplished to simple industry and perseverance. John Hunter said of himself, "My mind is like a beehive; but full as it is of buzz and apparent confusion, it is yet full of order and regularity, and food collected with incessant industry from the choicest stores of nature." We have, indeed, but to glance at the biographies of great men to find that the most distinguished inventors, artists, thinkers, and workers of all kinds, owe their success, in a great measure, to their indefatigable industry and application. They were men who turned all things to good--even time itself. Disraeli, the elder, held that the secret of success consisted in being master of your subject, such mastery being attainable only through continuous application and study. Hence it happens that the men who have most moved the world have not been so much men of genius, strictly so called, as men of intent mediocre abilities and untiring perseverance; not so often the gifted, of naturally bright and shining qualities, as those who have applied themselves diligently to their work, in whatsoever line that might lie. "Alas!" said a widow, speaking of her brilliant but careless son, "he has not the gift of continuance." Wanting in perseverance, such volatile natures are outstripped in the race of life by the diligent and even the dull.

Hence, a great point to be aimed at is to get the working quality well trained. When that is done, the race will be found comparatively easy. We must repeat and again repeat: facility will come with labor. Not even the simplest art can be accomplished without it; and what difficulties it is found capable of achieving! It was by early discipline and repetition that the late Sir Robert Peel cultivated those remarkable, though still mediocre, powers, which rendered him so illustrious an ornament of the British senate. When a boy at Drayton Manor, his father was accustomed to set him up at table to practice speaking extempore; and he early accustomed him to repeat as much of the Sunday's sermon as he could remember. Little progress was made at first, but by steady perseverance that habit of attention became powerful, and the sermon was at length repeated almost verbatim. When afterward replying in succession to the arguments of his parliamentary opponents--an art in which he was perhaps unrivaled--it was little surmised that the extraordinary power of accurate remembrance which he displayed on such occasions had been originally trained under the discipline of his father in the parish church of Drayton.

It is indeed marvelous what continuous application will effect in the commonest of things. It may seem a simple affair to play upon a violin; yet what a long and laborious practice it requires! Giardini said to a youth who asked him how long it would take to learn it, "Twelve hours a day for twenty years together."

Progress, however, of the best kind is comparatively slow. Great results cannot be achieved at once; and we must be satisfied to advance in life as we walk, step by step. De Maistre says that "To know *how to wait* is the great secret of success." We must sow before we can reap, and often have to wait long, content meanwhile to look patiently forward in hope: the fruit best worth waiting for often ripening the slowest. But "time and patience," says the Eastern proverb, "change the mulberry leaf to satin."

To wait patently, however, men must work cheerfully. Cheerfulness is an excellent working quality, imparting great elasticity to the character. As a bishop has said, "Temper is nine-tenths of Christianity;" so are cheerfulness and diligence nine-tenths of practical wisdom. They are the life and soul of success, as well as of happiness; perhaps the very highest pleasure in life consisting in clear, brisk, conscious working; energy, confidence, and every other good quality mainly depending upon it. Sydney Smith, when laboring as a parish priest at Foston-le-Clay, in Yorkshire--though he did not feel himself to be in his proper element--went cheerfully to work in the firm determination to do his best. "I am resolved," he said, "to like it, and reconcile myself to it, which is more manly than to feign myself above it, and to send up complaints by the post of being thrown away, and being desolate, and such like trash." So Dr. Hook, when leaving Leeds for a new sphere of labor, said, "Wherever I many be, I shall, by God's blessing, do with my might what my hand findeth to do; and if I do not fined work, I shall make it."

Laborers for the public good especially have to work long and patiently, often uncheered by the prospect of immediate recompense or result. The seeds they sow sometimes lie hidden under the winter's snow, and before the spring comes the husbandman may have gone to his rest. It is not every public worker who, like Rowland Hill, sees his great idea bring forth fruit in his lifetime. Adam Smith sowed the seeds of a great social amelioration in that dingy old University of Glasgow, where he so long labored, and laid the foundations of his "Wealth of Nations;" but seventy years passed before his work bore substantial fruits, nor indeed are they all gathered in yet.

Nothing can compensate for the loss of hope in a man: it entirely changes the character. "How can I work--how can I be happy," said a great but miserable thinker, "when I have lost all hope?" One of the most cheerful and courageous, because one of the most hopeful of workers, was Carey, the missionary. When in India, it was no uncommon thing for him to weary out three pundits, who officiated as his clerks in one day, he himself taking rest only in change of employment. Carey, the son of a shoemaker, was supported in his labors by Ward, the son of a carpenter, and

Marsham, the son of a weaver. By their labors a magnificent college was erected at Serampore; sixteen flourishing stations were established; the Bible was translated into sixteen languages, and the seeds were sown of a beneficent moral revolution in British India. Carey was never ashamed of the humbleness of his origin. On one occasion, when at the Governor-General's table, he overheard an officer opposite him asking another, loud enough to be heard, whether Carey had not once been a shoemaker: "No, sir," exclaimed Carey immediately; "only a cobbler." An eminently characteristic anecdote has been told of his perseverance as a boy. When climbing a tree one day, his foot slipped and he fell to the ground, breaking his leg by the fall. He was confined to his bed for weeks, but when he recovered and was able to walk without support, the very first thing he did was to go and climb that tree. Carey had need of this sort of dauntless courage for the great missionary work of his life, and nobly and resolutely he did it.

It was a maxim of Dr. Young, the philosopher, that "Any man can do what any other man has done;" and it is unquestionable that he himself never recoiled from any trials to which he determined to subject himself. It is related of him, that the first time he mounted a horse he was in company with the grandson of Mr. Barclay, of Ury, the well-known sportsman. When the horseman who preceded them leaped a high fence, Young wished to imitate him, but fell off his horse in the attempt. Without saying a word, he remounted, made a second effort, and was again unsuccessful, but this time he was not thrown farther than on to the horse's neck, to which he clung. At the third trial he succeeded, and cleared the fence.

The story of Timour, the Tartar, learning a lesson of perseverance under adversity from the spider is well know. Not less interesting is the anecdote of Audubon, the American ornithologist, as related by himself: "An accident," he says, "which happened to two hundred of my original drawings, nearly put a stop to my researches in ornithology. I shall relate it, merely to show how far enthusiasm--for by no other name can I call my perseverance--may enable the preserver of nature to surmount the most disheartening difficulties. I left the village of Henderson, in Kentucky, situated on the banks of the Ohio, where I resided for several years, to proceed to Philadelphia on business. I looked to my drawings before my departure, placed them carefully in a wooden box, and gave them in charge of a relative, with injunctions to see that no injury should happen to them. My absence was of several months; and when I returned, after having enjoyed the pleasures of home for a few days, I inquired after my box, and what I was pleased to call my treasure. The box was produced and opened; but, reader, feel for me--a pair of Norway rats had taken possession of the whole, and reared a young family among the gnawed bits of paper, which, but a month previous, represented nearly a thousand inhabitants of air! The burning heat which instantly rushed through my brain was too great to be endured without affecting my whole nervous system. I slept for several nights, and the days passed like days of oblivion--until the animal powers being recalled into action through the strength of my constitution, I took up my gun, my notebook and my pencils, and went forth to the woods as gayly as if nothing had happened. I felt pleased that I might now make better drawings than before; and ere a period not exceeding three years had elapsed, my portfolio was again filled."

The accidental destruction of Sir Isaac Newton's papers, by his little dog "Diamond" upsetting a lighted taper upon his desk, by which the elaborate calculations of many years were in a moment destroyed, is a well-known anecdote, and need not be repeated: it is said that the loss caused the philosopher such profound grief that it seriously injured his health, and impaired his understanding. An accident of a somewhat similar kind happened to the manuscript of Mr. Carlyle's first volume of his "French Revolution." He had lent the manuscript to a literary neighbor to peruse. By some mischance, it had been left lying on the parlor floor, and become forgotten. Weeks ran on, and the historian sent for his work, the printers being loud for "copy." Inquiries were made, and it was found that the maid-of- all-work, finding what she conceived to be a bundle of waste paper on the floor, had used it to light the kitchen and parlor fires with! Such was the answer returned to Mr. Carlyle; and his feelings can be imagined. There was, however, no help for him but to set resolutely to work to rewrite the book; and he turned to it and did it. He had no draft and was compelled to rake up from his memory, facts, ideas, and expressions which had been long since dismissed. The composition of the book in the first instance had been a work of pleasure; the rewriting of it a second time was one of pain and anguish almost beyond belief. That he persevered and finished the volume under such circumstances, affords an instance of determination of purpose which has seldom been surpassed.

There is no walk in life, in which success has been won, that has not its brilliant examples of the achievements of perseverance. The literary life, in which all who read are interested, has many illustrations of this. No great career affords stronger proof of this than that of the great Sir Walter Scott, who, delighting his own generation, must be honored by all the generations that follow.

His admirable working qualities were trained in a lawyer's office, where he pursued for many years a sort of drudgery scarcely above that of a copying clerk. His daily dull routine made his evenings, which were his own, all the ore sweet; and he generally devoted them to reading and study. He himself attributed to his prosaic office discipline that habit of steady, sober diligence, in which mere literary men are so often found wanting. As a copying clerk he was allowed 3 *d.* for every page containing a certain number of words; and he sometimes, by extra work, was able to copy as many as 120 pages in twenty-four hours, thus earning some 30 *s.*; out of which he would occasionally purchase an odd volume, otherwise beyond his means.

During his after-life Scott was wont to pride himself upon being a man of business, and he averred, in contradiction to what he called the cant of sonneteers, that there was no necessary connection between genius and an aversion or contempt for the common duties of life. On the contrary, he was of opinion that to spend some fair portion of every day in any matter-of-fact occupation was good for the higher faculties themselves in the upshot. While afterward acting as clerk to the Court of Session in Edinburgh, he performed his literary work chiefly before breakfast, attending the court during the day, where he authenticated registered deeds and writings of various kinds. "On the whole," says Lockhart, "it forms one of the most remarkable features in his history, that throughout the most active period of his literary career, he must have devoted a large proportion of his hours, during half at least of every year, to the conscientious discharge of professional duties." It was a principle of action which he laid down for himself, that he must earn his living by business, and not by literature. On one occasion he said, "I determined that literature should be my staff, not my crutch, and that the profits of my literary labor, however convenient otherwise, should not, if I could help it, become necessary to my ordinary expenses."

His punctuality was one of the most carefully cultivated of his habits, otherwise it had not been possible for him to get through so enormous an amount of literary labor. He mad it a rule to answer every letter received by him on the same day, except where inquiry and deliberation were requisite. Nothing else could have enabled him to keep abreast with the flood of communications that poured in upon him and sometimes put his good-nature to the severest test. It was his practice to rise by five o'clock and light his own fire. He shaved and dressed with deliberation, and was seated at his desk by six o'clock, with his papers arranged before him in the most accurate order, his works of reference marshaled round him on the floor, while at least one favorite dog lay watching his eye, outside the line of books. Thus by the time the family assembled for breakfast, between nine and ten, he had done enough--to use his own words--to break the neck of a day's work. But with all his diligent and indefatigable industry, and his immense knowledge, the result of may years' patient labor, Scott always spoke with the greatest diffidence of his own powers. On one occasion he said, "Throughout every part of my career I have felt pinched and hampered by my own ignorance."

But perseverance and effort do not always mean successful work. Freeman Hunt distinguishes admirably between activity and energy in the following statement, which it would be well to remember:

"There are some men whose failure to succeed in life is a problem to others, as well as to themselves. They are industrious, prudent, and economical; yet, after a long life of striving, old age finds them still poor. They complain of ill-luck; they say fate is against them. But the real truth is that their projects miscarry because they mistake mere activity for energy. Confounding two things essentially different, they suppose that if they are always busy, they must of a necessity be advancing their fortune; forgetting that labor misdirected is but a waste of activity."

"The person who would succeed in life is like a marksman firing at a target--if his shot misses the mark, it is but a waste of powder; to be of any service at all, it must tell in the bull's eye or near it. So, in the great game of life, what a man does must be made to count, or it had almost as well be left undone.

"The idle warrior, cut from a block of wood, who fights the air on the top of a weather-cock, instead of being made to turn some machine commensurate with his strength, is not more worthless than the merely active man who, though busy from sunrise to sunset, dissipates his labor on trifles, when he ought skillfully to concentrate it on some great end.

"Every person knows some one in his circle of acquaintance who, though always active, has this want of energy. The distemper, if we may call it such, exhibits itself in various ways. In some cases, the man has merely an executive faculty when he should have a directing one; in other words, he makes a capital clerk for himself, when he ought to do the thinking work for the establishment. In other cases, what is done is either not done at the right time, or not in the right way. Sometimes there is no distinction made between objects of different magnitudes, and as much labor is bestowed on a trivial affair as on a matter of great moment.

"Energy, correctly understood, is activity proportioned to the end. The first Napoleon would often, when in a campaign, remain for days without undressing himself, now galloping from point to point, now dictating dispatches, now studying maps and directing operations. But his periods of repose, when the crisis was over, were generally as protracted as his previous exertions had been. He has been known to sleep for eighteen hours without waking. Second-rate men, slaves of tape and routine, while they would fall short of the superhuman exertions of the great emperor, would have considered themselves lost beyond hope if they imitated what they call his indolence. They are capital illustrations of activity, keeping up their monotonous jog- trot for ever; while Napoleon, with his gigantic industry, alternating with such apparent idleness, is an example of energy.

"We do not mean to imply that chronic indolence, if relieved occasionally by spasmodic fits of industry, is to be recommended. Men who have this character run into the opposite extreme of that which we have been stigmatizing, and fail as invariably of securing success in life. To call their occasional periods of application energy, would be a sad misnomer. Such persons, indeed, are but civilized savages, so to speak; vagabonds at heart in their secret hatred of work, and only resorting to labor occasionally, like the wild Indian who, after lying for weeks about his hut, is roused by sheer hunger to start on a hunting excursion. Real energy is persevering, steady, disciplined. It never either loses sight of the object to be accomplished, or intermits its exertions while there is a possibility of success. Napoleon on the plains of Champagne, sometimes fighting two battles in one day, first defeating the Russians and then turning on the Austrians, is an illustration of this energy. The Duke of Brunswick, idling away precious time when he invaded France at the outbreak of the first Revolution, is an example of the contrary. Activity beats about a cover like an untrained dog, never lighting on the covey. Energy goes straight to the bird at once and captures it."

CHAPTER XVII
SUCCESS BUT SELDOM ACCIDENTAL.

A man may leap into sudden fortune at a bound, and without effort or foresight, but it is doubtful if any great permanent success ever was the outcome of blind chance.

The old adage, "Trust to luck," like many other adages that time has kept in unmerited circulation, is a bad one. The man who trusts to luck for his clothing is apt to wear rags, and he who depends on it for food is sure to go hungry.

We hear a great deal about the wonderful things that have been done by chance, but we seldom take the time to examine them. We read that sir Isaac Newton, sitting in his garden one day, "Chanced to see an apple fall to the ground," and this set him to thinking, and he discovered the laws of gravitation. New, ever since the first apple fell from the first tree in Eden, men have been watching that very commonplace occurrence. We might extend the field so as to embrace oranges, coconuts and all the fruits and nuts which, in every land and through all the long centuries of man's existence, have been falling to the ground--not by chance, however, yet they set no men to thinking, simply because not one of the millions of men who "chanced" to see the incident, "chanced" to have the reasoning powers of the great English scientist. If the apple, instead of falling to the ground, had shot up, without visible cause, to the sky, then the dullest observer would have wondered, even if he did not attempt to find an explanation. The falling of the apple in Newton's garden was not a chance, but an ordinary incident, which was made much of in the mind of an extraordinary man.

Watt "chanced" to see the lid of the kettle in his mother's kitchen lifted by the steam within, and this incident we are asked to believe was the origin of the engine invented by that great man. If no one else had ever witnessed a like phenomenon, then we might give some consideration to the element of chance. It was in the brain of Watt, and not in the lifting of the kettle lid, that the steam engine was born. There are no accidents in the progress of science.

In the same way, we are asked to believe that Galileo discovered the telescope, Whitney the cotton gin, and Howe the sewing machine.

But there have been some curious cases of chance fortune. A man out hunting in California made a mis-step and was plunged into a deep gulch in the Sierra Nevada. His gun was broken and he was sorely bruised, but he was more that repaid for the accident by the discovery of a rich gold mine at the bottom.

What would you think of the man, who, because of this, should shoulder a gun and go into the mountains, hoping to be precipitated into a gulch full of gold. If he started out for this purpose, of course, the element of chance would be eliminated, and yet that man would show just as much good sense as do the thousands who go through life--trusting to luck, and hoping for a miracle that never comes.

Success may be unforeseen, but it is a rare thing for it to come to the man who has not been preparing for it.

Lord Bacon well says: "Neither the naked hand nor the understanding, left to itself, can do much; the work is accomplished by instruments and helps, of which the need is not less for the understanding than the hand."

The Romans had a saying which is as true to-day as when first uttered: "Opportunity has hair in front, behind she is bald; if you seize her by the forelock, you may hold her, but if suffered to escape, not Jupiter himself can catch her again."

Accident does very little toward the production of any great result in life. Though sometimes what is called "a happy hit" may be made by a bold venture, the common highway of steady industry and application is the only safe road to travel. It is said of the landscape painter, Wilson, that when he had nearly finished a picture in a tame, correct manner, he would step back from it, his pencil fixed at the end of a long stick, and after gazing earnestly on the work, he would suddenly walk up and by a few bold touches give a brilliant finish to the painting. But it will not do for everyone who would produce an effect, to throw his brush at the canvas in the hope of producing a picture. The capability of putting in these last vital touches is acquired only by the labor of a life; and the probability is, that the artist who has not carefully trained himself beforehand, in attempting to produce a brilliant effect at a dash, will only produce a blotch.

Sedulous attention and painstaking industry always mark the true worker. The greatest men are not those who "despise the day of small things," but those who improve them the most carefully. Michael Angelo was one day explaining to a visitor at his studio what he had been doing to a statue since a previous visit. "I have retouched this part--polished that--softened this feature--brought out that muscle--given some expression to this lip, and more energy to that limb." "But these are trifles," remarked the visitor. "It may be so," replied the sculptor, "but recollect that trifles make perfection, and perfection is no trifle." So it was said of Nicolas Poussin, the painter, that the rule of his conduct was, that "whatever was worth doing at all was worth doing well;" and when asked, late in life, by his friend Vigneul de Marville, by what means he had gained so high a reputation among the painters of Italy, Poussin emphatically answered, "Because I have neglected nothing."

Although there are discoveries which are said to have been made by accident, if carefully inquired into it will be found that there has really been very little that was accidental about them. For the most part, these so-called accidents, have only been opportunities, carefully improved by genius. The brilliantly colored soap-bubbles blown through a common tobacco-pipe--though "trifles light as air" in most eyes--suggested to Dr. Young his beautiful theory of "interferences," and led to his discovery relating to the diffraction of light. Although great men are popularly supposed only to deal with great things, men such as Newton and Young were ready to detect the significance of the most familiar and simple facts; their greatness consisting mainly in their wise interpretation of them.

The difference between men consists, in a great measure, in the intelligence of their observation. The Russian proverb says of the nonobservant man, "He goes through the forest and sees no firewood." "The wise man's eyes are in his head," says Solomon, "but the fool walketh in darkness." "Sir," said Johnson on one occasion, to a fine gentleman just returned from Italy, "some men would learn more in the Hampstead stage than others in the tour of Europe." It is the mind that sees as well as the eye. Where unthinking gazers observe nothing, men of intelligent vision penetrate into the very fibre of the phenomena presented to them, attentively noting differences, making comparisons and recognizing their underlying idea. Many before Galileo had seen a suspended weight swing before their eyes with a measured beat, but he was the first to detect the value of the fact. One of the vergers in the cathedral at Pisa, after replenishing with oil a lamp which hung from the roof, left it swinging to and fro; and Galileo, then a youth of only eighteen, noting it attentively, conceived the idea of applying it to the measurement of time. Fifty years of study and labor, however, elapsed before he completed the invention of his Pendulum--the importance of which, in the measurement of time and in astronomical calculations, can scarcely be overrated. In like manner, Galileo, having casually heard that one Lippershey, a Dutch spectacle-maker, had presented to Count Maurice of Nassau an instrument by means of which distant objects appeared nearer to the beholder, addressed himself to the cause of such a phenomenon, which led to the invention of the telescope and proved the beginning of the modern science of astronomy. Discoveries such as these could never have been made by a negligent observer, or by a mere passive listener.

While Captain (afterward Sir Samuel) Brown was occupied in studying the construction of bridges, with the view of contriving one of a cheap description to be thrown across the Tweed near which he lived, he was walking in his garden one dewy autumn morning, when he saw a tiny spider's net suspended across his path. The idea immediately occurred to him, that a bridge of iron ropes or chains might be constructed in like manner, and the result was the invention of his suspension bridge. So James Watt, when consulted about the mode of carrying water by pipes under the Clyde, along the unequal bed of the river, turned his attention one day to the shell of a lobster presented at table; and from that model he invented an iron tube, which, when laid down, was found effectually to answer the purpose. Sir Isambard Brunel took his first lessons in forming the Thames Tunnel from the tiny shipworm: he saw how the little creature perforated the wood with its well-armed head, first in one direction and then in another, till the archway was complete, and then daubed over the roof and sides with a kind of varnish; and by copying this work exactly on a large scale, Brunel was at length enabled to construct his shield and accomplish his great engineering work.

It is the intelligent eye of the careful observer which gives these apparently trivial phenomena their value. So trifling a matter as the sight of seaweed floating past his ship, enabled Columbus to quell the mutiny which arose amongst his sailors at not discovering land, and to assure them that the eagerly sought New World was not far off.

It is the close observation of little things which is the secret of success in business, in art, in science, and in every pursuit in life. Human knowledge is but an accumulation of small facts, made by successive generations of men, the little bits of knowledge and experience carefully treasured up by them growing at length into a mighty pyramid. Though many of these facts and observations seemed in the first instance to have but slight significance, they are all found to have their eventual uses, and to fit into their proper places. Even many speculations seemingly remote, turn out to be the basis of results the most obviously practical. In the case of the conic sections discovered by Apollonius Pergaeus, twenty centuries elapsed before they were made the basis of astronomy--a science which enables the modern navigator to steer his way through unknown seas and traces for him in the heavens an unerring path to his appointed haven. And had not mathematicians toiled for so long, and, to uninstructed observers, apparently so fruitlessly, over the abstract relations of lines and surfaces, it is probably that but few of our mechanical inventions would have seen the light.

When Franklin made his discovery of the identity of lightning and electricity, it was sneered at, and people asked, "Of what use is it?" To which his reply was, "What is the use of a child? It may become a man!" When Galvani discovered that a frog's leg twitched when placed in contact with different metals, it could scarcely have been imagined that so apparently insignificant a fact could have led to important results. Yet therein lay the germ of the electric telegraph, which binds the intelligence of continents together, and, probably before many years have elapsed will "put a girdle round the globe." So, too, little bits of stone and fossil, dug out of the earth, intelligently interpreted, have issued in the science of geology and the practical operations of mining, in which large capitals are invested and vast numbers of persons profitably employed.

The gigantic machinery employed in pumping our mines, working our mills and manufactories, and driving our steamships and locomotives, in like manner depends for its supply of power upon so slight an agency as little drops of water expanded with heat--that familiar agency called steam, which we see issuing from that common tea-kettle spout, but which, when pent up within an ingeniously contrived mechanism, displays a force equal to that of millions of horses, and contains a power to rebuke the waves and set even the hurricane at defiance. The same power at work within the bowels of the earth has been the cause of those volcanoes and earthquakes which have played so mighty a part in the history of the globe.

This art of seizing opportunities and turning even accidents to account, bending them to some purpose, is a great secret of success. Dr. Johnson has defined genius to be "a mind of large general powers accidentally determined in some particular direction." Men who are resolved to find a way for themselves, will always find opportunities enough; and if they do not lie ready to their hand, they will make them. It is not those who have enjoyed the advantages of colleges, museums, and public galleries, that have accomplished the most for science and art; nor have the greatest mechanics and inventors been trained in mechanics' institutes. Necessity, oftener than facility, has been the mother of invention; and the most prolific school of all has been the school of difficulty. Some of the very best workmen have had the most indifferent tools to work with. But it is not tools that make the workman, but the trained skill and perseverance of the man himself. Indeed it is proverbial that the bad workman never yet had a good tool. Some one asked Opie by that wonderful process he mixed his colors. "I mix them with my brains, sir," was his reply. It is the same with every workman who would excel. Ferguson made marvelous things--such as his wooden clock, that accurately measured the hours-- by means of a common penknife, a tool in everybody's hand; but then everybody is not a Ferguson. A pan of water and two thermometers were the tools by which Dr. Black discovered latent heat; and a prism, a lens and a sheet of pasteboard enable Newton to unfold the composition of light and the origin of colors. An eminent foreign *savant* once called upon Dr. Wollaston, and requested to be shown over his laboratories, in which science had been enriched by so many important discoveries, when the doctor took him into a little study, and, pointing to an old tea-tray on the table, containing a few watch-glasses, test-papers, a small balance, and a blowpipe, said, "There is all the laboratory I have!"

Stothard learnt the art of combining colors by closely studying butterflies' wings: he would often say that no one knew what he owed to those tiny insects. A burnt stick and a barn door served Wilkie in lieu of pencil and canvas. Bewiek first practiced drawing on the cottage walls of his native village, which he covered with his sketches in chalk; and Benjamin Watt made his first brushes out of the cat's tail.

Ferguson laid himself down in the fields at night in a blanket, and made a map of the heavenly bodies by means of a thread with small beads on it stretched between his eye and the stars. Franklin first robbed the thundercloud of its lightning by means of a kite made with two cross-sticks and a silk handkerchief. Watt made his first model of the condensing steam-engine out of an old anatomist's syringe, used to inject the arteries previous to dissection. Gifford worked his first problems in mathematics, when a cobbler's apprentice, upon small scraps of leather, which he beat smooth for the purpose; whilst Rittenhouse, the astronomer, first calculated eclipses on his plow handle.

The most ordinary occasions will furnish a man with opportunities or suggestions for improvement, if he be but prompt to take advantage of them. Professor Lee was attracted to the study of Hebrew by finding a Bible in that tongue in a synagogue, while working as a common carpenter at the repair of the benches. He became possessed with a desire to read the book in the original, and, buying a cheap second- hand copy of a Hebrew grammar, he set to work and learned the language for himself. As Edmund Stone said to the Duke of Argyle, in answer to his grace's inquiry how he, a poor gardener's boy, had contrived to be able to read Newton's Principia in the Latin, "One needs only to know the twenty-four letters of the alphabet in order to learn everything else that one wishes." Application and perseverance, and the diligent improvement of opportunities, will do the rest.

The attention of Dr. Priestley, the discoverer of so many gases, was accidentally drawn to the subject of chemistry through his living in the neighborhood of a brewery. When visiting the place one day, he noted the peculiar appearances attending the extinction of lighted chips in the gas floating over the fermented liquor. He was forty years old at the time, and knew nothing of chemistry. He consulted books to ascertain the cause, but they told him little, for as yet nothing was known on the subject. Then he began to experiment, with some rude apparatus of his own contrivance. The curious results of his first experiments led to others, which in his hands shortly became the science of pneumatic chemistry. About the same time, Scheele was obscurely working in the same direction in a remote Swedish village; and he discovered several new gases, with no more effective apparatus at his command than a few apothecaries' vials and pigs' bladders.

Sir Humphry Davy, when an apothecary's apprentice, performed his first experiments with instruments of the rudest description. He extemporized the greater part of them himself, out of the motley materials which chance threw in his way- -to pots and pans of the kitchen, and the vials and vessels of his master's surgery. It happened that a French ship was wrecked off the Land's End, and the surgeon escaped, bearing with him his case of instruments, amongst which was an old-fashioned clyster apparatus; this article he presented to Davy, with whom he had become acquainted. The apothecary's apprentice received it with great exultation, and forthwith employed it as a part of a pneumatic apparatus which he contrived, afterward using it to perform the duties of an air-pump in one of his experiments on the nature and sources of heat.

In like manner, professor Faraday, Sir Humphry Davy's scientific successor, made his first experiments in electricity by means of an old bottle, while he was still a working bookbinder. And it is a curious fact, that Faraday was first attracted to the study of chemistry by hearing one of Sir Humphry Davy's lectures on the subject at the Royal Institution. A gentleman, who was a member, calling one day at the shop where Faraday was employed in binding books, found him pouring over the article "Electricity," in an encyclopedia placed in his hands to bind. The gentleman, having made inquiries, found that the young bookbinder was curious about such subjects, and gave him an order of admission to the Royal Institution, where he attended a course of four lectures delivered by Sir Humphry. He took notes of them, which he showed to the lecturer, who acknowledged their scientific accuracy, and was surprised when informed of the humble position of the reporter. Faraday then expressed his desire to devote himself to the prosecution of chemical studies, from which Sir Humphry at first endeavored to dissuade him: but the young man persisting, he was at length taken into the Royal Institution as an assistant; and eventually the mantle of the brilliant apothecary's boy fell upon the worthy shoulders of the equally brilliant bookbinder's apprentice.

The words which Davy entered in his notebook, when about twenty years of age, working in Dr. Beddoes' laboratory at Bristol, were eminently characteristic of him: "I have neither riches, nor power, nor birth to recommend me; yet if I live I trust I shall not be of less service to mankind and my friends, than if I had been born with all these advantages." Davy possessed the capability, as Faraday did, of devoting the whole power of his mind to the practical and experimental investigation of a subject in all its bearings; and such a mind will rarely fail, by dint of mere industry and patient thinking, in producing results of the highest order. Coleridge said of Davy: "There is an energy and elasticity in his mind, which enables him to seize on and analyze all questions, pushing them to their legitimate consequences. Every subject in Davy's mind has the principle of vitality. Living thoughts spring up like turf under his feet." Davy, on his part said of Coleridge, whose abilities he greatly admired: "With the most exalted genius, enlarged views, sensitive heart, and enlightened mind, he will be the victim of a want of order, precision, and regularity."

It is not accident, then, that helps a man in the world so much as purpose and persistent industry. To the feeble, the sluggish and purposeless, the happiest accidents will avail nothing--they pass them by, seeing no meaning in them. But it is astonishing how much can be accomplished if we are prompt to seize and improve the opportunities for action and effort which are constantly presenting themselves. Watt taught himself chemistry and mechanics while working at his trade of a mathematical instrument maker, at the same time that he was learning German from a Swiss dyer. Stephenson taught himself arithmetic and mensuration while working as an engine-man, during the night shifts; and when he could snatch a few moments in the intervals allowed for meals during the day, he worked his sums with a bit of chalk upon the sides of the colliery wagons. Dalton's industry was the habit of his life. He began from his boyhood, for he taught a little village school when he was only about twelve years old--keeping the school in winter, and working upon his father's farm in summer. He would sometimes urge himself and companions to study by the stimulus of a bet, though bred a Quaker; and on one occasion by his satisfactory solution of a problem, he won as much as enabled him to buy a winter's store of candles. He continued his meteorological observations until a day or two before he died--having made and recorded upward of 200,000 in the course of his life.

With perseverance, the very odds, and ends of time may be worked up into results of the greatest value. An hour in every day withdrawn from frivolous pursuits would, if profitably employed, enable a person of ordinary capacity to go far toward mastering a science. It would make an ignorant man a well-informed one in less than ten years. Time should not be allowed to pass without yielding fruits, in the form of something learnt worthy of being known, some good principle culti-vated, or some good habit strengthened. Dr. Mason Good translated Lucretuis while riding in his carriage in the streets of London, going the round of his patients. Dr. Darwin composed nearly all his works in the same way while driving about in his "sulky" from house to house in the country ==writing down his thoughts on little scraps of paper, which he carried about with him for the purpose. Hale wrote his "Contemplations" while traveling on circuit. Dr. Burney learnt French and Italian while traveling on horseback from one musical pupil to another in the course of his profession. Kirke White learnt Greek while walking to and fro from a lawyer's office; and we personally know a man of eminent position who learnt Latin and French while going messages as an errand-boy.

Hugh Miller was a busy man of observant faculties, who studied literature as well as science, with zeal and success. The book in which he has told the story of his life("My Schools and Schoolmasters"), is extremely interesting, and calculated to be eminently useful. It is the history of the formation of a truly noble character in the humblest condition of life, and inculcates most powerfully the lessons of self-help, self-respect, and self- dependence. While Hugh was but a child, his father, who was a sailor, was drowned at sea, and he was brought up by his widowed mother. He had a school training after a sort, but his best teachers were the boys with whom he played, the men amongst whom he lived. He read much and miscellaneously, and picked up odd sorts of knowledge from many quarters--from workmen, car-penters, fishermen and sailors, and above all, from the old boulders strewed along the shores of the Cromarty Firth. With a big hammer which had belonged to his great-grandfather, an old buccaneer, the boy went about chipping the stones, and accumulating specimens of mica, porphyry, garnet, and such like. Sometimes he had a day in the woods, and there, too, the boy's attention was excited by the pecu-liar geological curiosities which came in his way. While searching among the rocks on the beach, he was sometimes asked, in irony, by the farm-servants who came to load their carts with sea-weed, whether he "was gettin' siller in the stanes," but was so unlucky as never to be able to answer in the affirmative. When of a suitable age he was apprenticed to the trade of his choice--that of a working stone-mason; and he began his laboring career in a quarry looking out upon the Cromarty Firth. This quarry proved one of his best schools. The remarkable geological formations which it displayed awakened his curiosity. The bar of deep-red stone beneath, and the bar of pale-red clay above, were noted by the young quarryman, who even in such unpromising subjects, found matter of observation and reflection. Where other men saw nothing, he detected analogies, differences, and peculiarities which set him a-thinking. He simply kept his eyes and his mind open; was sober, diligent and persevering; and this was the secret of his intellectual growth.

His curiosity was excited and kept alive by the curious organic remains, principally of old and extinct species of fishes, ferns, and ammonites, which were revealed along the coast by the washings of the waves, or were exposed by the stroke of his mason's hammer. He never lost sight of the subject, but went on accumulating observations and comparing formations, until at length, many years afterward, when no longer a working mason, he gave to the world his highly interesting work on the "Old Red Sandstone," which at once established his reputation as a scientific geologist. But this work was the fruit of long years of patient observation and research. As he modestly states in his autobiography, "The only merit to which I lay claim in the case is that of patient research--a merit in which whoever wills may rival or surpass me; and this humble faculty of patience, when rightly developed, may lead to more extraordinary development of ideas than even genius itself."

"Chance," said an old Vermont farmer, "is like going into a field with a pail, and waiting for a cow to come to you and back up to be milked."

"Shun delays, they breed remorse;

Take thy time while time is lent thee; Creeping snails have weakest force, Fly their fault, lest thou repent thee;

Good is best when sooner wrought,
Ling'ring labors come to nought.
"Hoist up sail while gale doth last,
Tide and wind stay no man's pleasure! Seek not time when time is past,
Sober speed is wisdom's leisure;
After-wits are dearly bought,
Let thy fore-wit guide thy thought.
"Time wears all his locks before,
Take thou hold upon his forehead;

When he flees he turns no more,
And behind his scalp is naked.
Works adjourn'd have many stays,
Long demurs breed new delays."

CHAPTER XVIII
CULTIVATE OBSERVATION AND JUDGMENT.

L ook before you leap," old Commodore Vanderbilt used to say. "I like active men, but I have no use for the fellow who is so much in earnest that he goes off half-cocked." We all know the danger of a gun that goes off half-cocked, but it is not so apt to bring disaster as is the man who goes off without due preparation.

It is fortunate for us that we cannot see into the future, but the Father who has kept from us the gift of prophecy has blessed us with a foresight and judgment that enable us to see pretty accurately what must be the inevitable consequence of certain acts.

The power to observe carefully and judge accurately is a rare gift, but it is one that can be cultivated. The ancients had a motto "Know thyself," and the great poet Pope tells us that "the proper study of mankind is man." A knowledge of human nature is invaluable in every life-calling that brings us into contact with our fellows, and this can be gained only by careful observation.

Stephen Girard attributed much of his success to his "ability to read men at a glance." And so carefully did the great merchant prince, Alexander T, Stewart, study this, that it is said he rarely made a mistake in the character of a man he took into his employ.

Cultivate observation. Oliver Wendell Holmes maintained that all the difference in men, no matter their callings, lay in the difference of their ability to observe and draw proper conclusions from their observations. Professor Huxley says that "observation is the basis of all our scientific knowledge." And Andrew Carnegie attributes his great success to his cultivation of this faculty.

Every young man, ambitious to win--and what young man worthy the name is not?--should have a standard of excellence for himself, and then he should care-fully study and observe the methods of the men who he admires or with whom he is brought into contact. It is the ability to do this that constitutes the difference between the man drudge and the man anxious to assume greater responsibilities by mastering his necessary duties.

In a lecture to young men on this subject, Henry Ward Beecher said:

"The young should begin life with a standard of excellence before them, to which they should readily conform themselves. There should be a fixed determina-tion to make the best of one's self, in whatever circumstances we may be placed. Let the young man determine that whatever he undertakes he will do well; that he will make himself master of the business upon which he enters, and always prepare himself for advancement by becoming worthy of it. It is not opportunity of rising which is wanting, so much as the ability to rise. It is not the patronage of friends and the outward helps of fortune, to which the prominent men of our country owe their elevation, either in wealth or influence, so much as to their own vigorous and steady exertions. We hear a great many complaints, both among young men and old, of the favoritism of fortune, and the partiality of the world; but observation leads us to believe that, to a very great extent, those who deserve promotion ob-tain it. Those who are worthy of confidence will have confidence reposed in them. Those who give evidence of ability and industry will find opportunity enough for their exercise."

Take a familiar illustration. A young man engages in some business, and is, in ever respect, a beginner in life. A common education is all that he possesses. He knows almost nothing of the world, and very little of the occupation on which he has entered. He performs his duty from day to day sufficiently well, and does what he is expected to do. But it does not enter into his mind to do anything beyond what is required, nor to enlarge his capacities by reading or reflection. He is, at the best, a steady plodding man, who will go forward, if at all, very slowly, and will rise, if at all, to no great elevation. He is not the sort of person who is looked for to oc-cupy a higher position. One opportunity of advancement after another may come directly within his reach, and he asks the influence of friends to help him to secure it. They give their aid feebly, because they have no great hopes of success, and are not confident of their own recommendation. As a matter of course, some one else, more competent or more in earnest, steps in before him, and then we hear renewed complaints of favoritism and injustice. Such a one may say in his defense that he has been guilty of no dereliction of duty; that no fault has been found with him, and that, therefore, he was entitled to advancement. But this does not follow. Something more that that may reasonably be required. To bestow increased confidence, we require the capacity and habit of improvement in those whom we employ. The man who is entitled to rise is one who is always enlarging his capacity, so that he is evidently able to do more that he is actually doing.

In every department of business, whether mechanical or mercantile, or whatever it may be, there is a large field of useful knowledge which should be carefully explored. An observing eye and an inquiring mind will always find enough for examination and study. It may not seem to be of immediate use--it may have nothing to do with this week's or this year's duty--yet it is worth knowing. The mind gains greater skillfulness by the intelligence which directs it.

The result is all the difference between a mere drudge and an intelligent workman; between the mere salesman or clerk and the enterprising merchant; between the obscure and pettifogging lawyer and the sagacious, influential counselor. It is the difference between one who deserves to be, and will be, stationary in the world, and one who, having determined to make the best of himself, will continually rise in influence and true respectability. This whole difference we may see every day among those who have enjoyed nearly equal opportunities. We may allow something for what are called the accidents of social influence, and the turns of fortune. But, after all fair allowance has been made, we shall find that the great cause of difference is in the men themselves. Let the young man who is beginning life put away from him all notions of advancement without desert. A man of honorable feelings will not even desire it. He will ever shrink from engaging in duties which he is not able fairly to perform. He will, first of all, secure to himself the capacity of performing them, and then he is ready for them whenever they come.

Without observation and judgment there can be no permanent advance. Without observation, experience has no value, and the passing years add nothing to our fund of useful knowledge. Judgment is the ability to weigh these observations, and use them for our own protection or advancement.

Not only in business, but in science and art, observation and good judgment are necessary. Excellence in art, as in everything else, can only be achieved by dint of painstaking labor and a close observation of those whom we regard as our superiors. There is nothing less accidental than the painting of a fine picture, or the chiseling of a noble statue. Every skilled touch of the artist's brush or chisel, though guided by genius, is the product of unremitting study. Sir Joshua Reynolds was such a believer in the force of industry, that he held that artistic excellence, "however expressed by genius, taste, or the gift of heaven may be acquired." Writing to Barry he said, "Whoever is resolved to excel in painting, or indeed any other art, must bring all his mind to bear upon that one object from the moment that he rises till he goes to bed." And on another occasion he said, "Those who are resolved to excel must go to their work, willing or unwilling, morning, noon, and, night: they will find it no play, but very hard labor." But although diligent application is no doubt absolutely necessary for the achievement of the highest distinction in art, it is equally true that, without the inborn genius, no amount of mere industry, however well applied, will make an artist. The gift comes by nature, but is perfected by self-culture, which is of more avail that all the imparted learning of the schools. But even genius without good judgment may be an unbroken steed without a bridle.

All great artists and authors have been famed for their powers of observation; indeed, it is claimed that it is this power that distinguishes them from other men.

No matter how generous nature has been in bestowing the gift of genius, the pursuit of art is nevertheless a long and continuous labor. Many artists have been precocious, but without diligence their precocity would have come to nothing. The anecdote related of West is well known. When only seven years old, struck with the beauty of the sleeping infant of his eldest sister, whilst watching by its cradle, he ran to seek some paper, and forthwith drew its portrait in red and black ink. The little incident revealed the artist in him, and it was found impossible to draw him from his bent. West might have been a greater painter had he not been injured by too early success: his fame, though great, was not purchased by study, trials and difficulties, and it has not been enduring.

Richard Wilson, when a mere child, indulged himself with tracing figures of men and animals on the walls of his father's house with a burnt stick. He first directed his attention to portrait painting; but when in Italy, calling one day at the house of Zucarelli, and growing weary with waiting, he began painting the scene on which his friend's chamber window looked. When Zucarelli arrived, he was so charmed with the picture that he asked if Wilson had not studied landscape, to which he replied that he had not. "Then I advise you," said the other, "to try; for you are sure of great success." Wilson adopted the advice, studied and worked hard, and became the first great English landscape painter.

Sir Joshua Reynolds, when a boy, forgot his lessons, and took pleasure only in drawing, for which his father was accustomed to rebuke him. The boy was destined for the profession of physic, but his strong instinct for art could not be repressed, and he became a painter. Gainsborough went sketching, when a schoolboy, in the woods of Sudbury, and at twelve he was a confirmed artist; he was a keen observer and a hard worker--no picturesque feature of any scene he had once looked upon escaping his diligent pencil. William Blake, a hosier's son, employed himself in drawing designs on the backs of his father's shop-bills, and making sketches on the counter. Edward Bird, when a child only three or four years old, would mount a chair and draw figures on the walls, which he called French and English soldiers. A box of colors was purchased for him, and his father, desirous of turning his love of art to account, put him apprentice to a maker of teatrays! Out of this trade he gradually raised himself, by study and labor, to the rank of a Royal Academician.

Hogarth, though a very dull boy at his lessons, took pleasure in making drawings of the letters of the alphabet, and his school exercises were more remarkable for the ornaments with which he embellished them, than for the matter of the exercises themselves. In the latter respect he was beaten by all the blockheads of the school, but in his adornments he stood alone. His father put him apprentice to a silversmith, where he learnt to draw, and also to engrave spoons and forks with crests and ciphers. From silver-chasing he went on to teach himself engraving on copper, principally griffins and monsters of heraldry, in the course of which practice he became ambitious to delineate the varieties of human character. The singular excellence which he reached in this art was mainly the result of careful observation and study. He had the gift, which he sedulously cultivated, of committing to memory the precise features of any remarkable face, and afterward reproducing them on paper; but if any singularly fantastic form or odd face came in his way, he would make a sketch of it on the spot upon his thumbnail, and carry it home to expand at his leisure. Everything fantastical and original had a powerful attraction for him, and he wandered into many out-of-the-way places for the purpose of meeting with character. By this careful storing of his mind, he was afterward enabled to crowd an immense amount of thought and treasure observation into his works. Hence it is that Hogarth's pictures are so truthful a memorial of the character, the manners, and even the very thoughts of the times in which he live. True painting, he himself observed, can only be learnt in one school, and that is kept by Nature. But he was not a highly cultivated man, except in his own walk. His school education had been of the slenderest kind, scarcely even perfecting him in the art of spelling; his self-culture did the rest. For a long time he was in very straitened circumstances, but nevertheless worked on with a cheerful heart. Poor though he was, he contrived to live within his small means, and he boasted with becoming pride, that he was "a punctual paymaster." When he had conquered all his difficulties and become a famous and thriving man, he loved to dwell upon his early labors and privations, and to fight over again the battle which ended so honorably to him as a man and so gloriously as an artist. "I remember the time," said he on one occasion, "when I have gone moping into the city with scarce a shilling, but as soon as I have received ten guineas there for a plate, I have returned home, put on my sword, and sallied out with all the confidence of a man who had thousands in his pockets."

Perhaps there is no living man of eminence who so well and forcibly illustrates these qualities of judgment and observation as that greatest of living American inventors, Thomas A. Edison.

Mr. Edison, as we have already stated, had only a few weeks at school in his whole life. He was born in the upper part of New York State in 1847. His parents were poor, and early in life, to use his own expressive words, he "had to start out and hustle." One would think that selling newspapers on a railroad train was not a calling that afforded any educational advantages, but to the man of observation there is no position in life, whether in the busy haunts of men or the silence of the wilderness, that is not replete with valuable information if we but know where to look for it, and have the judgment to use it after it is obtained.

Through the favor of the telegraph operator, whose child's life he had saved when the little one was nearly under the wheels of a train, young Edison was enabled to study telegraphy. During this apprenticeship, if such it may be called, the boy not only learned how to send and receive a message, so as to fit himself for the position of operator, but he learned all about the mechanism and the batteries of the instrument he operated.

"Nothing escaped Tom Edison's observation," said a man who knew him at this time. "He saw everything, and he not only saw it, but he set about learning its whys and wherefores, and he stuck at it till he had learned all there was to be learned about it."

Said another friend, "I've known Edison since he was a boy of fourteen, and of my own knowledge I can say he never spent an idle day in his life. Often when he should have been asleep I have known him to sit up half the night reading. He did not take to novels or wild Western adventures, but read works on mechanics, chemistry and electricity, and he mastered them, too. But in addition to his reading, which he could only indulge at odd hours, he carefully cultivated his wonderful powers of observation, till at length, when he was not actually asleep, it may be said he was learning all the time. Schools and colleges are all very well, but Mr. Edison's career goes to show that a man may become famous, prosperous, and well educated, if he has the necessary capacity for observing and weighing."

Another illustrious example of the same kind is the late George W. Childs, of Philadelphia. He was born in Baltimore, Md., in 1829, and at the age of twelve he had to begin the battle of life by taking the position of errand boy in a book store. "I had no schooling," he said, when speaking of his early struggles, "but I had a quenchless thirst for information. I had no tine to read the books I had to handle and carry sometimes in a wheelbarrow, but I kept my eyes and ears open. I studied the binding and manufacture, though I had not the slightest idea of the contents; and from these early observations I made up my mind that one day I would become a publisher on my own account."

How successfully Mr. Childs did this, we all know. While yet in his teens, he made his way, without money or friends, to Philadelphia, and found a place in a book store, where the same method of education by observation was continued.

The first time he saw a copy of the Philadelphia *Ledger*, a time when he had scarcely the penny to spare that bought it, he made up his mind that one day he would own that paper--and he carried out his resolution.

So excellent was his judgment that not only publishers, but statesmen and bankers sought it. From the humblest beginnings George W. Childs rose up and up till the greatest men of two continents rejoiced in his friendship, and his name was on the lips of all who admire a noble life devoted to philanthropic deeds.

Our American biographies are full of examples of self-taught men--men who have become educated through observation, and great through good judgment and increasing effort, but there are not many of them that commend themselves so warmly to the heart as the life of the good, wise, and generous George W. Childs.

CHAPTER XIX
SINGLENESS OF PURPOSE.

We have all heard of the "Jack of all trades, and master of none." Such men never win, though they may excite the admiration of the curious by their impractical versatility.

In early times, even in the early settlement of our own country, it was necessary for not only men, but women also, to be many-sided in their capacity for work; but the world's swift advance has made this unnecessary. A farmer can now buy shoes cheaper than he could make them at home, and the farmer's wife has no longer to learn the art of spinning and weaving.

A French philosopher in speaking of this subject says: "It is well to know something about everything, and everything about something." That is general information is always useful, but special information is essential to special success.

The field of learning is too vast to be carefully gone over in one lifetime, and the business world is too extensive to permit any man to become acquainted with all its topography. A man may do a number of things fairly well, but he can do only one thing very well.

Often versatility instead of being a blessing is an injury. A few men like Michael Angelo in art, Benjamin Franklin in science and letters, and Peter Cooper in various departments of manufacture have succeeded in everything they undertook, but to hold these up as examples to be followed would be to make a rule of an exception.

Singleness of purpose is one of the prime requisites of success. Fortune is jealous, and refuses to be approached from all sides by the same suitor.

We have known men of marked ability, but want of purpose, who studied for the ministry and failed; who then studied law--and failed. After this they tried medicine and journalism, only to fail in each; whereas, had they stuck resolutely to one thing success would not have been uncertain.

A young man may not be able at the very start to hit upon the vocation for which he is best adapted, but should he find it, he will see that his ability to avail himself of its advantages will depend largely on the energy and singleness of purpose displayed in the work for which he had no liking.

There is a famous speech recorded of an old Norseman, thoroughly characteristic of the Teuton. "I believe neither in idols nor demons," said he; "I put my sole trust in my own strength of body and soul." The ancient crest of a pickaxe with the motto of "Either I will find a way or make one," was an expression of the same sturdy independence which to this day distinguishes the descendants of the Northmen. Indeed, nothing could be more characteristic of the Scandinavian mythology, than that it had a god with a hammer. A man's character is seen in small matters; and from even so slight a test as the mode in which a man wields a hammer, his energy may in some measure be inferred. Thus an eminent Frenchman hit off in a single phrase the characteristic quality of the inhabitants of a particular district, in which a friend of his proposed to settle and buy land. "Beware," said he, "of making a purchase there; I know the men of that Department; the pupils who come from it to our veterinary school at Paris *do not strike hard upon the anvil*; they want energy; and you will not get a satisfactory return on any capital you may invest there."

Hugh Miller said the only school in which he was properly taught was "that world-wide school in which toil and hardship are the severe but noble teachers." He who allows his application to falter, or shirks his work on frivolous pretexts, is on the sure road to ultimate failure. Let any task be undertaken as a thing not possible to be evaded, and it will soon come to be performed with alacrity and cheerfulness. Charles IX of Sweden was a firm believer in the power of will, even in youth. Laying his hand on the head of his youngest son when engaged on a difficult task, he exclaimed, "He *shall* do it! he *shall* do it!" The habit of application becomes easy in time, like every other habit. Thus persons with comparatively moderate powers will accomplish much, if they apply themselves wholly and indefatigably to one thing at a time. Fowell Buxton placed his confidence in ordinary means and extraordinary application; realizing the Scriptural injunction, "Whatsoever thy hand findeth to do, do it with thy might;" and he attributed his own success in life to his practice of "being a whole man to one thing at a time."

"Where there is a will there is a way," is an old and true saying. He who re-solves upon doing a thing, by that very resolution often scales the barriers to it, and secures its achievement. To think we are able, is almost to be so--to determine upon attainment is frequently attainment itself. Thus, earnest resolution has often seemed to have about it almost a savor of omnipotence. The strength of Suwarrow's character lay in his power of willing, and, like most resolute persons, he preached it up as a system. "You can only half will," he would say to people who failed. Like Richelieu and Napoleon, he would have the word "impossible" banished from the dictionary. "I don't know," "I can't," and "impossible," were words which he de-tested above all others. "Learn! Do! Try!" he would exclaim. His biographer has said of him, that he furnished a remarkable illustration of what may be effected by the energetic development and exercise of faculties the germs of which at least are in every human heart.

One of Napoleon's favorite maxims was, "The truest wisdom is a resolute de-termination." His life, beyond most others, vividly showed what a powerful and unscrupulous will could accomplish. He threw his whole force of body and mind direct upon his work. Imbecile rulers and the nations they governed went down before him in succession. He was told that the Alps stood in the way of his armies. "There shall be no Alps," he said, and the road across the Simplon was constructed, through a district formerly almost inaccessible. "Impossible," said he, "is a word only to be found in the dictionary of fools." He was a man who toiled terribly; sometimes employing and exhausting four secretaries at a time. He spared no one, not even himself. His influence inspired other men, and put a new life into them. "I made my generals out of mud" he said. But all was of no avail; for Napoleon's intense selfish-ness was his ruin, and the ruin of France, which he left a prey to anarchy.

Before the man resolutely impelled to action by singleness of purpose, every obstacle disappears as he approaches, and every lesson of experience becomes the stepping-stone to further victories in the same direction.

It is this singleness of purpose, this absorption in a great life- work, that nerves our missionaries in their exile. A splendid example of this is presented in the career of the great missionary and explorer, Dr. Livingstone.

He has told the story of his life in that modest and unassuming manner which is so characteristic of the man himself. His ancestors were poor but honest High-landers, and it is related of one of them, renowned in his district for wisdom and prudence, that when on his death-bed, he called his children round him and left them these words, the only legacy he had to bequeath: "In my lifetime," said he, "I have searched most carefully through all the traditions I could find of our family, and I never could discover that there was a dishonest man among our forefathers; if, therefore, any of you, or any of your children, should take to dishonest ways, it will not be because it runs in our blood; it does not belong to you: I leave this precept with you--Be honest." At the age of ten, Livingstone was sent to work in a cotton factory near Glasgow as a "piecer." With part of his first week's wages he bought a Latin grammar, and began to learn that language, pursuing the study for years at a night-school. He would sit up conning his lessons till twelve or later, when not sent to bed by his mother, for he had to be up and at work in the factory every morning by six. In this way he plodded through Virgil and Horace, also reading extensively all books, excepting novels, that came in his way, but more especially scientific works and books of travels. He occupied his spare hours, which were but few, in the pursuit of botany, scouring the neighborhood to collect plants. He even carried on his reading amidst the roar of the factory machinery, so placing the book upon the spinning-jenny which he worked, that he could catch sentence after sentence as he passed it. In this way the persevering youth acquired much useful knowledge; and as he grew older, the desire possessed him of becoming a missionary to the heathen. With this object he set himself to obtain a medical education, in order the better to be qualified for the work. He accordingly economized his earnings, and saved as much money as enabled him to support himself while attending the Medical and Greek classes as well as the Divinity Lectures, at Glasgow, for several winters, working as a cotton-spinner during the remainder of each year. He thus supported himself, during his college career, entirely by his own earnings as a factory work-man, never having received a farthing of help from any other source. "Looking back now," he honestly said, "at that life of toil, I cannot but feel thankful that it formed such a material part of my early education; and, were it possible, I should like to be-gin life over again in the same lowly style, and to pass through the same hardy train-ing." At length he finished his medical curriculum, wrote his Latin thesis, passed his examinations, and was admitted a licentiate of the Faculty of Physicians and

Surgeons. At first he thought of going to China, but the war then waging with that country prevented his following out the idea; and having offered his services to the London Missionary Society, he was by them sent out to Africa, which he reached in 1840. He had intended to proceed to China by his own efforts; and he says the only pang he had in going to Africa at the charge of the London Missionary Society was, because "it was not quite agreeable to one accustomed to worked his own way to become, in a manner, dependent upon others." Arrived in Africa, he set to work with great zeal. He could not brook the idea of merely entering upon the labors of others, but cut out a large sphere of independent work, preparing himself for it by undertaking manual labor in building and other handicraft employment, in addition to teaching, which, he says, "made me generally as much exhausted and unfit for study in the evenings as ever I had been when a cotton-spinner." Whilst laboring amongst the Bechuanas, he dug canals, built houses, cultivated fields, reared cattle, and taught the natives to work as well as to worship. When he first started with a party of them on foot upon a long journey, he overheard their observations upon his appearance and powers. "He is not strong," said they; "he is quite slim, and only appears stout because he puts himself into those bags (trousers): he will soon knock up." This caused the missionary's Highland blood to rise, and made him despise the fatigue of keeping them all at the top of their speed for days together, until he heard them expressing proper opinions of his pedestrian powers. What he did in Africa, and how he worked, may be learnt from his own "Missionary Travels," one of the most fascinating books of its kind that has ever been given to the public. One of his last known acts is thoroughly characteristic of the man. The "Birkenhead" steam launch, which he took out with him to Africa, having proved a failure, he sent home orders for the construction of another vessel at an estimated cost of 2,000 pounds. This sum he proposed to defray out of the means which he had set aside for his children, arising from the profits of his books of travel. "The children must make it up themselves," was in effect his expression in sending home the order for the appropriation of the money.

The career of John Howard was throughout a striking illustration of the same power of patient purpose. His sublime life proved that even physical weakness could remove mountains in the pursuit of an end recommended by duty. The idea of ameliorating the condition of prisoners engrossed his whole thoughts, and possessed him like a passion; and no toil, or danger, nor bodily suffering could turn him from that great object of his life. Though a man of no genius and but moderate talent, his heart was pure and his will was strong. Even in his own time he achieved a remarkable degree of success; and his influence did not die with him, for it has continued powerfully to affect not only the legislation of his own country, but of all civilized nations, down to the present hour.

Horace Mann, famous as a teacher and reformer in his day, was urged by his friends in Ohio to go to Congress. He replied: "I have a great deal of respect for men in public life, but I have more respect for my on life-work. If I know anything, it is the science or art of teaching, and to this work, please God, I shall devote the whole of my life." And he kept his word.

Singleness of purpose implies firmness, for in this day of change and speculation, the young man who has saved up a little money, hoping one day to go into business for himself, will find on every hand temptations to invest in enterprises of which he knows nothing. Here his resolution will be tested. Remember there is no element of human character so potential for weal or woe as firmness. To the merchant and the man of business it is all-important. Before its irresistible energy the most formidable obstacles become as cobweb barriers in its path. Difficulties, the terror of which causes the timid and pampered sons of luxury to shrink back with dismay, provoke from the man a lofty determination only a smile. The whole history of our race--all nature, indeed--teems with examples to show what wonders may be accomplished by resolute perseverance and patient toil.

It is related of Tamerlane, the terror of whose arms spread through all the Eastern nations, and whom victory attended at almost every step, that he once learned from an insect a lesson of perseverance, which had a striking effect on his future character and success.

When closely pursued by his enemies, as a contemporary writer tells the incident, he took refuge in some old ruins, where left to his solitary musings, he espied an ant tugging and striving to carry a single grain of corn. His unavailing efforts were repeated sixty-nine times, and at each brave attempt, as soon as he reached a certain point of projection, he fell back with his burden, unable to surmount it; but the seventieth time he bore away his spoil in triumph, and left the wondering hero reanimated and exulting in the hope of future victory.

How pregnant the lesson this incident conveys! How many thousand instances there are in which inglorious defeat ends the career of the timid and desponding, when the same tenacity of purpose would crown it with triumphant success.

Resolution is almost omnipotent. It was well observed by a heathen moralist, that it is not because things are difficult that we dare not undertake them. Be, then, bold in spirit. Indulge no doubts. Shakespeare says truly and wisely--

"Our doubts are traitors, And make us lose the good we oft might win, By fearing to attempt."

In the practical pursuit of our high aim, let us never lose sight of it in the slightest instance; for it is more by a disregard of small things, than by open and flagrant offenses, that men come short of excellence. There is always a right and a wrong; and, if you ever doubt, be sure you take not the wrong. Observe this rule, and every experience will be to you a means of advancement.

CHAPTER XX
BUSINESS AND BRAINS.

Many, prompted no doubt by a feeling of envy, are apt to sneer at the culture and mental ability of the men who have won in business. "Dumb luck," "mean plodding," "the robbery of employees," these and other reasons are assigned by the unreasoning and uncharitable for the prosperity of men who won with fewer advantages than themselves.

Every student of the world's progress knows that business men have done even more than great authors for the advance of civilization. And we all know, though the world is apt to kneel to military idols, that inventors have done far more than have soldiers for the good of humanity.

The man who succeeds in commerce, trade, or manufactures, thereby shows a foresight and executive ability that would surely have commanded success in any other calling. Men who know books and nothing else are apt to imagine that the merchant, whose life is devoted to facts, figures, and results, must by reason of that be wanting in the higher intellectual faculties. Nor is this belief wholly confined to authors in America.

Hazlitt, in one of his clever essays, represents the man of business as a mean sort of person put in a go-cart, yoked to a trade or profession; alleging that all he has to do is, not to go out of the beaten track, but merely to let his affairs take their own course. "The great requisite," he says, "for the prosperous management of ordinary business is the want of imagination, or of any ideas but those of custom and interest on the narrowest scale." but nothing could be more one-sided, and in effect untrue, than such a definition. Of course, there are narrow-minded men of business, as there are narrow-minded scientific men, literary men and legislators; but there are also business men of large and comprehensive minds, capable of action on the very largest scale. As Burke said in his speech on the India bill, he knew statesmen who were peddlers, and merchants who acted in the spirit of statesmen.

If we take into account the qualities necessary for the successful conduct of any important undertaking--that it requires special aptitude, promptitude of action on emergencies, capacity for organizing the labor often of large numbers of men, great tact and knowledge of human nature, constant self-culture, and growing experience in the practical affairs of life--it must, we think, be obvious that the school of business is by no means so narrow as some writers would have us believe. Mr. Helps spoke much nearer the truth when he said that consummate men of business are as rare almost as great poets--rarer, perhaps, than veritable saints and martyrs. Indeed, of no other pursuit can it so emphatically be said, as of this, that "business makes men."

It has, however, been a favorite fallacy with dunces in all times that men of genius are unfitted for business, as well as that business occupations unfit men for the pursuits of genius. The unhappy youth who committed suicide a few years since because he had been "born to be a man and condemned to be a grocer," proved by the act that his soul was not equal even to the dignity of grocer. For it is not the calling that degrades the man, but the man that degrades the calling. All work that brings honest gain is honorable, whether it be of hand or mind. The fingers may be soiled, yet the heart remain pure; for it is not material so much as moral dirt that defiles--greed far more than grime, and vice than verdigris.

The greatest have not disdained to labor honestly and usefully for a living, though at the same time aiming after higher things. Thales, the first of the seven sages; Solon, the second founder of Athens, and Hyperates, the mathematician, were all traders. Plato, called the Divine by reason of the excellence of his wisdom, defrayed his traveling expenses in Egypt by the profits derived from the oil which he sold during his journey. Spinoza maintained himself by polishing glasses while he pursued his philosophical investigations. Linnaeus, the great botanist, prosecuted his studies while hammering leather and making shoes. Shakespeare was the successful manager of a theatre--perhaps priding himself more upon his practical qualities in that capacity than on his writing of plays and poetry. Pope was of opinion that Shakespeare's principal object in cultivating literature was to secure an hones independence. Indeed, he seems to have been altogether indifferent to literary reputation. It is not known that he superintended the publication of a single play, or even sanctioned the printing of one; and the chronology of his writings is still a mystery. It is certain, however, that he prospered in his business, and realized sufficient to enable him to retire upon a competency to his native town of Stratford-upon-Avon.

Chaucer was in early life a soldier, and afterward an effective Commissioner of Customs, and Inspector of Woods and Crown Lands. Spenser was secretary to the Lord Deputy of Ireland, was afterward Sheriff of Cork, and is said to have been shrewd and attentive in matters of business. Milton, originally a schoolmaster, was elevated to the post of Secretary to the Council of State during the Commonwealth; and the extant Order-book of the Council, as well as many of Milton's letters which are preserved, give abundant evidence of his activity and usefulness in that office. Sir Isaac Newton proved himself an efficient Master of the Mint, the new coinage of 1694 having been carried on under his immediate personal superintendence. Cowper prided himself upon his business punctuality, though he confessed that he "never knew a poet, except himself, that was punctual in anything." But against this we may set the lives of Wordsworth and Scott--the former a distributor of stamps, the latter a clerk to the Court of Session--both of whom, though great poets, were eminently punctual and practical men of business. David Ricardo, amidst the occupations of his daily business as a London stock- jobber, in conducting which he acquired an ample fortune, was able to concentrate his mind upon his favorite subject--on principles of political economy; for he united in himself the sagacious commercial man and the profound philosopher. Baily, the eminent astronomer, was another stock-broker; and Allen, the chemist, was a silk manufacturer.

We have abundant illustrations, in our own day, of the fact, that the highest intellectual power is not incompatible with the active and efficient performance of routine duties. Grote, the great historian of Greece, was a London banker. And it is said that when John Stuart Mill, one of the greatest modern thinkers, retired from the Examiner's office of an important company, he carried with him the admiration and esteem of his fellow-officers, not on account of his high views of philosophy, but because of the high standard of efficiency which he had established in his office, and the thoroughly satisfactory manner in which he had conducted the business of his department.

The path of success in business is usually the path of common sense. Patient labor and application are as necessary here as in the acquisition of knowledge or the pursuit of science. The old Greeks said, "To become an able man in any profession, three things are necessary--nature, study, and practice." In business, practice, wisely and diligently improved, is the great secret of success. Some may make what are called "lucky hits," but like money earned by gambling, such "hits" may only serve to lure one to ruin. Bacon was accustomed to say that it was in business as in ways--the nearest way was commonly the foulest, and that if a man would go the fairest way he must go somewhat about. The journey may occupy a longer time, but the pleasure of the labor involved by it, and the enjoyment of the results produced, will be more genuine and unalloyed. To have a daily appointed task of even common drudgery to do makes the rest of life feel all the sweeter.

One of the best illustrations we know of, of great natural abilities winning great success in mechanical fields is the career of the now famous Andrew Carnegie, of Pennsylvania.

This remarkable man was born in Scotland in 1835. When ten years of age, his parents, who were poor, moved to Pittsburg. Then, as now, there were excellent public schools in the "Smoky City," but young Carnegie was not able to avail himself of their advantages, as he desired to do. While still in his teens he found employment in running a stationary engine. He did his work well, and every moment not required by his engine was devoted to study.

Before the youth had seen a practical keyboard, he had mastered the principles of telegraphy, and succeeded, by reason of the knowledge obtained in this way, in getting a position as an operator. At that time all messages were read from rolls of paper, on which the Morse characters were indented; but Andrew Carnegie, while still under twenty-one, was the first operator in the world to demonstrate, that to a skillful man the roll was unnecessary. He learned to read by sound then, as all operators do now. What scholar will say that a high order of intellect was not involved in this achievement?

"Hard work, close observation, strict economy, and the determination to give my employer the best that was in me, without regard to the compensation, these were my impelling motives in those early days, and to these I attribute all the prosperity with which Heaven has blessed me." This is what Mr. Carnegie says of himself, and his words are full of encouragement and inspiration to the young man who has the same obstacles to overcome.

"It is not what you make, but what you save that brings wealth." Mr. Carnegie discovered this early in life, and while he helped his parents like a dutiful son, he never spent an unnecessary cent on himself.

"I was too busy working and studying to contract the habits that make such inroads on the health and pockets of young men," says Mr. Carnegie, "and this helped me in many ways."

While still young he had an opportunity to invest his savings in the first sleeping car, invented by Woodruff, and out of this he got his first good start.

Active, industrious, and quick to foresee results, he took an interest in the oil discoveries of Pennsylvania, and with such success that from the profits he was enabled to organize the greatest series of rolling mills and foundries in the world.

Mr. Carnegie is still in the prime of life. He has spent several fortunes in good works, and is still a very rich as he is certainly a highly honored man. But the point we wish to make is that Mr. Carnegie is a fine example of the high order of intellect necessary for the greatest success in the business world.

Although self-educated, Mr. Carnegie is an author of world-wide reputation. His work "Triumphant Democracy" is splendid vindication of the institutions of his adopted country. "He knows more about books," says one who knows Mr. Carnegie well, "than half the authors, and he can find himself in no society where he does not find himself the peer of the best."

Those who fail in life are, however, very apt to assume a tone of injured innocence, and conclude to hastily that everybody excepting themselves has had a hand in their personal misfortunes. An eminent writer lately published a book, in which he described his numerous failures in business, naively admitting, at the same time, that he was ignorant of the multiplication-table; and he came to the conclusion that the real cause of his ill-success in life was the money-worshiping spirit of the age. Lamartine also did not hesitate to profess his contempt for arithmetic; but, had it been less. probably we should not have witnessed the unseemly spectacle of the admirers of that distinguished personage engaged in collecting subscriptions for his support in his old age.

Again, some consider themselves born to ill-luck, and make up their minds that the world invariably goes against them without any fault on their own part. We have heard of a person of this sort who went so far as to declare his belief that if he had been a hatter, people would have been born without heads! There is, however, a Russian proverb which says that Misfortune is next door to Stupidity; and it will often be found that men who are constantly lamenting their ill- luck, are in some way reaping the consequences of their own neglect, mismanagement, improvidence, or want of application. Dr. Johnson, who came up to London with a single guinea in his pocket, and who once accurately described himself in his signature to a letter addressed to a noble lord, as Impransus, or Dinnerless, has honestly said, "All the complaints which are made of the world are unjust; I never knew a man of merit neglected; it was generally by his own fault that he failed of success."

Did you ever think of the intellectual qualifications essential to the successful business man? No? well, it would be very difficult to name such a qualification which the business man cannot make available.

Attention, application, accuracy, method, punctuality and dispatch, are the principal qualities required for the efficient conduct of business of any sort. These, at first sight, may appear to be small matters; and yet they are of essential importance to human happiness, well-being, and usefulness. They are little things, it is true; but human life is made up of comparative trifles. It is the repetition of little acts which constitutes not only the sum of human character, but which determines the character of nations. And where men or nations have broken down, it will almost invariably be found that neglect of little things was the rock on which they split. Every human being has duties to be performed, and, therefore, has need of cultivating the capacity for doing them; whether the sphere of action be the management of a household, the conduct of a trade or profession, or the government of a nation.

In addition to the ordinary working qualities, the business man of the highest class requires quick perception and firmness in the execution of his plans. Tact is also important; and though this is partly the gift of nature, it is yet capable of being cultivated and developed by observation and experience. Men of this quality are quick to see the right mode of action, and if they have decision of purpose, are prompt to carry out their undertakings to a successful issue. These qualities are especially valuable, and indeed indispensable, in those who direct the action of other men on a large scale, as for instance, in the case of the commander of an army in the field. It is not merely necessary that the general should be great as a warrior, but also as a man of business. He must possess great tact, much knowledge of character, and ability to organize the movements of a large mass of men, whom he has to feed, clothe, and furnish with whatever may be necessary in order that they may keep the field and win battles. In these respects Napoleon and Wellington were both first-rate men of business.

Not only does business require the highest order of intellect, but successful business men, particularly in America, have been the patrons of the arts and sciences and the founders of great schools. The prosperity of Princeton is largely due to Marquand and Bonner. the great Cooper Institute for the free education of poor boys and girls, in the applied arts and sciences, will endure as long as New York city, as a monument to the intellectual forethought and noble munificence of Peter Cooper. Girard College, in Philadelphia, which yearly sends out hundreds of young men--orphans on entrance, but admirable fitted to work their way in life--is a refutation of the charge that successful business men do not appreciate culture.

Lehigh University was founded by Judge Asa Packer, of Mauch Chunk, who began life as a canal-boat man. Lafayette College, Easton, points with pride to Pardee Hall, the gift of a man who began the life- battle without money or friends. Vanderbilt University, Stanford University, and scores of great schools go to prove that the great business men who endowed them, were not indifferent to culture and the needs of higher education.

Yes, business requires brains, and the better the brains and the more thorough their training, the greater the assurance of success.

CHAPTER XXI
PUT MONEY IN THY PURSE HONESTLY.

How a man uses money--makes it, saves it, and spends it--is perhaps one of the best tests of practical wisdom," says Mr. Smiles. Although money ought by no means to be regarded as a chief end of man's life, neither is it a trifling matter, to be held in philosophic contempt, representing, as it does, to so large an extent, the means of physical comfort and social well-being. Indeed, some of the finest qualities of human nature are intimately related to the right use of money; such as generosity, honesty, justice, and self-sacrifice; as well as the practical virtues of economy and providence. On the other hand, there are their counterparts of avarice, fraud, injustice, and selfishness, as displayed by the inordinate lovers of gain; and the vices of thriftlessness, extravagance, and improvidence, on the part of those who misuse and abuse the means entrusted to them. "So that," as is wisely observed by Henry Taylor in his thoughtful "Notes from Life," "an right measure and manner of getting, saving, spending, giving, taking, lending, borrowing, and bequeathing, would almost argue a perfect man."

Comfort in worldly circumstances is a condition which every man is justified in striving to attain by all worthy means. It secures that physical satisfaction which is necessary for the culture of the better part of his nature; and enables him to provide for those of his own household, without which, says the apostle, a man is "worse than an infidel." Nor ought the duty to be any the less pleasing to us, that the respect which our fellow-men entertain for us in no slight degree depends upon the manner in which we exercise the opportunities which present themselves for our honorable advancement in life. The very effort required to be made to succeed in life with this object, is of itself an education: stimulating a man's sense of self-respect, bringing out his practical qualities, and disciplining him in the exercise of patience, perseverance, and such like virtues. The provident and careful man must necessarily be a thoughtful man, for he lives not merely for the present, but with provident forecast makes arrangements for the future. He must also be a temperate man, and exercise the virtue of self-denial, than which nothing is so much calculated to give strength to the character. John Sterling says truly, that "the worst education which teaches self-denial, is better than the best which teaches everything else and not that." The Romans rightly employed the same word (virtus) to designate courage, which is in a physical sense what the other is in moral; the highest virtue of all being victory over ourselves.

Hence the lesson of self-denial--the sacrificing of a present gratification for a future good--is one of the last that is learnt. Those classes which work the hardest might naturally be expected to value the most the money which they earn. Yet the readiness with which so many are accustomed to eat up and drink up their earnings as they go, renders them, to a great extent, dependent upon the frugal.

Men of business are accustomed to quote the maxim that "Time is money;" but it is more; the proper improvement of it is self-culture, self-improvement, and growth of character. An hour wasted daily on trifles or in indolence, would, if devoted to self-improvement, make an ignorant man wise in a few years, and, employed in good works, would make his life fruitful, and death a harvest of worthy deeds. Fifteen minutes a day devoted to self-improvement, will be felt at the end of the year. Good thoughts and carefully gathered experience take up no room, and may be carried about as our companions everywhere, without cost or encumbrance. An economical use of time is the true mode of securing leisure: it enables us to get through business and carry it forward, instead of being driven by it. On the other hand, the miscalculation of time involves us in perpetual hurry, confusion, and difficulties; and life becomes a mere shuffle of expedients, usually followed by disaster. Nelson once said, "I owe all my success in life to having been always a quarter of an hour before my time."

Some take no thought of the value of money until they have come to an end of it, and many do the same with their time. The hours are allowed to flow by unemployed, and then when life is fast waning, they bethink themselves of the duty of making a wiser use of it. But the habit of listlessness and idleness may already have become confirmed, and they are unable to break the bonds with which they have permitted themselves to become bound. Lost wealth may be replaced by industry, lost knowledge by study, lost health by temperance or medicine, but lost time is gone forever.

A proper consideration of the value of time will also inspire habits of punctuality. "Punctuality," said Louis XIV, "is the politeness of kings." It is also the duty of gentlemen, and the necessity of men of business. Nothing begets confidence in a man sooner than the practice of this virtue, and nothing shakes confidence sooner than the want of it. He who holds to his appointment and does not keep you waiting for him, shows that he has regard for your time as well as for his own. Thus punctuality is one of the modes by which we testify our personal respect for those whom we are called upon to meet in the business of life. It is also conscientiousness, in a measure; for an appointment is a contract, expressed or implied, and he who does not keep it breaks faith, as well as dishonestly uses other people's time, and thus inevitably loses character. We naturally come to the conclusion that the person who is careless about time is careless about business, and that he is not the one to be trusted with the transaction of matters of importance. When Washington's secretary excused himself for the lateness of his attendance and laid the blame upon his watch, his master quietly said, "Then you must get another watch, or I another secretary."

The person who is negligent of time and its employment is usually found to be a general disturber of others' peace and serenity. It was wittily said by Lord Chesterfield of the old Duke of Newcastle--"His Grace loses an hour in the morning, and is looking for it all the rest of the day." Everybody with whom the unpunctual man has to do is thrown from time to time into a state of fever: he is systematically late; regular only in his irregularity. He conducts his dawdling as if upon system; arrives at his appointment after time; gets to the railway station after the train has started; posts his letter when the box has closed. Thus business is thrown into confusion, and everybody concerned is put out of temper.

To secure independence, the practice of simple economy is all that is necessary. Economy requires neither superior courage nor eminent virtue; it is satisfied with ordinary energy, and the capacity of average minds. Economy, at bottom, is but the spirit of order applied in the administration of domestic affairs: it means management, regularity, prudence, and the avoidance of waste. The spirit of economy was expressed by our Divine Master in the words, "Gather up the fragments that remain, so that nothing may be lost." His omnipotence did not disdain the small things of life; and even while revealing His infinite power to the multitude, he taught the pregnant lesson of carefulness, of which all stand so much in need.

Economy also means to power of resisting present gratification for the purpose of securing a future good, and in this light it represents the ascendancy of reason over the animal instincts. It is altogether different from penuriousness: for it is economy that can always best afford to be generous. It does not make money an idol, but regards it as a useful agent. As Dean Swift observes, "we must carry money in the head, not in the heart." Economy may be styled the daughter of Prudence, the sister of Temperance, and the mother of Liberty. It is eminently conservative- -conservative of character, of domestic happiness, and social well-being. It is, in short, the exhibition of self-help in one of its best forms.

Francis Horner's father gave him this advice on entering life: "Whilst I wish you to be comfortable in every respect, I cannot too strongly inculcate economy. It is a necessary virtue to all; and however the shallow part of mankind may despise it, it certainly leads to independence, which is a grand object to every man of a high spirit."

Every man ought to contrive to live within his means. This practice is of the very essence of honesty. For if a man does not manage honestly to live within his own means, he must necessarily be living dishonestly upon the means of somebody else. Those who are careless about personal expenditure, and consider merely their own gratification, without regard for the comfort of others, generally find out the real uses of money when it is too late. Though by nature generous, these thriftless persons are often driven in the end to do very shabby things. They waste their money as they do their time; draw bills upon the future; anticipate their earnings; and are thus under the necessity of dragging after them a load of debts and obligations, which seriously affect their actions as free and independent men.

It was a maxim of Lord Bacon, that when it was necessary to economize, it was better to look after petty savings than to descend to petty gettings. The loose cash which many persons throw away uselessly, and worse, would often form a basis of fortune and independence for life. These wasters are their own worst enemies, though generally found amongst the ranks of those who rail a the injustice of "the world." But if a man will not be his own friend, how can he expect that others will be. Orderly men of moderate means have always something left in their pockets to help others; whereas, your prodigal and careless fellows who spend all, never find an opportunity for helping anybody. It is poor economy, however, to be a scrub. Narrow-mindedness in living and in dealing is generally short- sighted, and leads to failure. Generosity and liberality, like honesty, always prove the best policy af- ter all. Though Jenkinson, in the "Vicar of Wakefield," cheated his kind-hearted neighbor Flamborough in one way or another every year, "Flamborough," said he, "has been regularly growing in riches, while I have come to poverty and a jail." And practical life abounds in cases of brilliant results from a course of generous and honest policy.

The proverb says that "an empty bag cannot stand upright;" neither can a man who is in debt. It is also difficult for a man who is in debt to be truthful; hence, it is said that lying rides on debt's back. The debtor has to frame excuses to his creditor for postponing payment of the money he owes him, and probably also to contrive falsehoods. It is easy enough for a man who will exercise a healthy resolution, to avoid incurring the first obligation; but the facility with which that has been in- curred often becomes a temptation to a second; and very soon the unfortunate bor- rower becomes so entangled that no late exertion of industry can set him free. The first step in debt is like the first step in falsehood; almost involving the necessity of proceeding in the same course, debt following debt, as lie follows lie. Haydon, the painter, dated his decline fro the day on which he first borrowed money. He realized the truth of the proverb, "Who goes a-borrowing, goes a-sorrowing." The significant entry in his diary is: "Here began debt and obligation, out of which I have never been and never shall be extricated as long as I live." His autobiography shows but too painfully how embarrassment in money matters produces poignant distress of mind, utter incapacity for work, and constantly recurring humiliations. The written advice which he gave to a youth when entering the navy was as fol- lows: "Never purchase any enjoyment if it cannot be procured without borrowing of others. Never borrow money; it is degrading. I do not say never lend, but never lend if by lending you render yourself unable to pay what you owe; but under any circumstances never borrow." Fichte, the poor student, refused to accept even pres- ents from his still poorer parents.

Dr. Johnson held that early debt is ruin. His words on the subject are weighty, and worthy of being held in remembrance. "Do not," said he, "accustom yourself to consider debt only as an inconvenience; you will find it a calamity. Poverty takes away so many means of doing good, and produces so much inability to resist evil, both natural and moral, that it is by all virtuous means to be avoided. . . . Let it be your first care, then, not to be in any man's debt. Resolve not to be poor; whatever you have, spend less. Poverty is a great enemy to human happiness; it certainly destroys liberty, and makes some virtues impracticable and others extremely difficult. Frugality is not only the basis of quiet, but of beneficence. No man can help others that wants help himself; we must have enough before we have to spare."

It is the bounden duty of every man to look his affairs in the face, and to keep an account of his incomings and outgoings in money matters. The exercise of a little simple arithmetic in this way will be found of great value. Prudence requires that we shall pitch our scale of living a degree below our means, rather than up to them. But this can only be done by carrying out faithfully a plan of living by which both ends may be made to meet. John Locke strongly advised this course: "Nothing," said he, "is likelier to keep a man within compass than having constantly before his eyes the state of his affairs in a regular course of account." The Duke of Wellington kept an accurate detailed account of all the moneys received and expended by him. "I make a point," said he to Mr. Gleig, "of paying my own bills, and I advise every one to do the same; formerly I used to trust a confidential servant to pay them, but I was cured of that folly by receiving one morning, to my great surprise, duns of a year or two's standing. The fellow had speculated with my money, and left my bills unpaid." Talking of debt, his remark was, "It makes a slave of a man. I have often known what it was to be in want of money, but I never got into debt." Washington was as particular as Wellington was, in matters of business detail; and it is a remarkable fact, that he did not disdain to scrutinize the smallest outgoings of his household-- determined as he was to live honestly within his means--even when holding the high office of President of the United States.

There is a dreadful ambition abroad for being "genteel." We keep up appearances, too often at the expense of honesty; and though we may not be rich yet we must seem to be so. We must be "respectable," though only in the meanest sense--in mere vulgar outward show. We have not the courage to go patiently onward in the condition of life in which it has pleased God to call us; but must needs live in some fashionable state to which we ridiculously please to call ourselves, and to gratify the vanity of that unsubstantial genteel world of which we form a part. There is a constant struggle and pressure for front streets in the social amphitheatre; in the midst of which all noble self-denying resolve is trodden down, and many fine natures are inevitably crushed to death. What waste, what misery, what bankruptcy come from all this ambition to dazzle others with the glare of apparent worldly success, we need not describe.

The young man, as he passes through life, advances through a long line of tempters ranged on either side of him; and the inevitable effect of yielding is degradation in a greater or a less degree. Contact with them tends insensibly to draw away from him some portion of the divine electric element with which his nature is charged; and his only mode of resisting them is to utter and act out his "No" manfully and resolutely. He must decide at once, not waiting to deliberate and balance reasons; for the youth, like "the woman who deliberates, is lost." Many deliberate, without deciding; but "not to resolve, *is* to resolve." A perfect knowledge of man is in the prayer, "Lead us not into temptation." But temptation will come to try the young man's strength; and once yielded to, the power to resist grows weaker and weaker. Yield once, and an element of virtue has gone. Resist manfully, and the first decision will give strength for life; repeated it will become a habit. It is in the outworks of the habits formed in early life that the real strength of the defense must lie; for it has been wisely ordained that the machinery of moral existence should be carried on principally through the medium of the habits, so as to save the wear and tear of the great principles within. It is good habits which insinuate themselves into the thousand inconsiderable acts of life, that really constitute by far the greater part of man's moral conduct.

Many popular books have been written for the purpose of communicating to the public the grand secret of making money. But there is no secret whatever about it, as the proverbs of every nation abundantly testify. "Take care of the pennies and the pounds will take care of themselves." "Diligence is the mother of good luck." "No pains, no gains." "No sweat, no sweet." "Work and thou shalt have." "The world is his who has patience and industry." "Better go to bed supperless than rise in debt." Such are specimens of the proverbial philosophy, embodying the hoarded experience of many generations, as to the best means of thriving in the world. They were current in people's mouths long before books were invented; and like other popular proverbs they were the first codes of popular morals. Moreover, they have stood the test of time, and the experience of every day still bears witness to their accuracy, force, and soundness. The Proverbs of Solomon are full of wisdom as to the force of industry, and the use and abuse of money: "He that is slothful in work is brother to him that is a great waster." "Go to the ant, thou sluggard; consider her ways, and be wise." Poverty, says the preacher, shall come upon the idler, "as one that traveleth, and want as an armed man;" but of the industrious and upright, "the hand of the diligent maketh rich." "the drunkard and the glutton shall come to poverty; and drowsiness shall clothe a man with rags." "Seest thou a man diligent in his business? he shall stand before kings." But above all, "It is better to get wisdom than gold; for wisdom is better than rubies, and all the things that may be desired are not to be compared to it."

Simple industry and thrift will go far toward making any person of ordinary working faculty comparatively independent in his means. Even a working man may be so, provided he will carefully husband his resources, and watch the little outlets of useless expenditure. A penny is a very small matter, yet the comfort of thousands of families depends upon the proper spending and saving of pennies. If a man allows the little pennies, the results of his hard work, to slip out of his fingers--some to the beer-shop, some this way and some that--he will find that his life is little raised above one of mere animal drudgery. On the other hand, if he take care of the pennies-- putting some weekly into a benefit society or an insurance fund, others into a savings' bank, and confiding the rest to his wife to be carefully laid out, with a view to the comfortable maintenance and education of his family--he will soon find that this attention to small matters will abundantly repay him, in increasing means, growing comfort at home, and a mind comparatively free from fears as to the future. And if a working man have high ambition and possess richness in spirit--a kind of wealth which far transcends all mere worldly possessions--he may not help himself, but be a profitable helper of others in his path through life.

While credit is the soul of trade, improperly used it is the death of business. No man should run into debt for a luxury, and every prudent man will have money in his purse for life's necessities. Remember, the man who is in debt without seeing his way out is a slave. Speaking of this Jacob Abbott says:

"There is, perhaps, nothing which so grinds the human soul, and produces such an insupportable burden of wretchedness and despondency, as pecuniary pressure. Nothing more frequently drives men to suicide; and there is, perhaps, no danger to which men in an active and enterprising community are more exposed. Almost all are eagerly reaching forward to a station in life a little above what they can well afford, or struggling to do a business a little more extensive than they have capital or steady credit for; and thus they keep, all through life, *just above* their means--and just above, no matter by how small an excess, is inevitable misery.

"Be sure, then, if your aim is happiness, to bring down, at all hazards, your style of living, and your responsibilities of business, to such a point that you shall easily be able to reach it. Do this, I say, at all hazards. If you cannot have money enough for your purpose in a house with two rooms, take a house with one. It is your only chance for happiness. For there is such a thing as happiness in a single room, with plain furniture and simple fare; but there is no such thing as happiness with responsibilities which cannot be met, and debts increasing without any prospect of their discharge."

"After I had earned my first thousand dollars by the hardest kind of work," said Commodore Vanderbilt, "I felt richer and happier than when I had my first million. I was out of debt, every dollar was honestly mine, and I saw my way to success."

CHAPTER XXII
A SOUND MIND IN A SOUND BODY.

Gibons, the historian, says: "Every person has two educations--one which he receives from others, and one, the most important, which he gives to himself." "The best part of every man's education," said Sir Walter Scott, "is that which he gives to himself." The late Sir Benjamin Brodie delighted to remember this saying, and he used to congratulate himself on the fact that professionally he was self-taught. But this is necessarily the case with all men who have acquired distinction in letters, science, or art. The education received at school or college is but a beginning, and is valuable mainly inasmuch as it trains the mind and habituates it to continuous application and study. That which is put into us by others is always far less ours than that which we acquire by our own diligent and persevering effort. Knowledge conquered by labor becomes a possession--a property entirely our own. A greater vividness and permanency of impression is secured; and facts thus acquired become registered in the mind in a way that mere imparted information can never effect. This kind of self-culture also calls forth power and cultivates strength. The solution of one problem helps the mastery of another; and thus knowledge is carried into faculty. Our own active effort is the essential thing; and no facilities, no books, no teachers, no amount of lessons learnt by rote, will enable us to dispense with it.

The best teachers have been the readiest to recognize the importance of self-culture, and of stimulating the student to acquire knowledge by the active exercise of his own faculties. They have relied more upon *training* than upon *telling*, and sought to make their pupils themselves active parties to the work in which they were engaged; thus making teaching something far higher than the mere passive reception of the scraps and details of knowledge. This was the spirit in which the great Dr. Arnold worked; he strove to teach his pupils to rely upon themselves, and develop their powers by their own active efforts, himself merely guiding, directing, stimulating, and encouraging them. "I would far rather," he said, "send a boy to Van Diemen's Laud, where he must work for his bread, than send him to Oxford to live in luxury, without any desire in his mind to avail himself of his advantages." "If there be one thing on earth," he observed on another occasion, "which is truly admirable, it is to see God's wisdom blessing an inferiority of natural powers, when they have been honestly, truly, and zealously cultivated." Speaking of a pupil of this character, he said, "I would stand to that man hat in hand." Once at Laleham, when teaching a rather dull boy, Arnold spoke somewhat sharply to him, on which the pupil looked up in his face and said, "Why do you speak angrily, sir? *indeed*, I am doing the best I can." Years afterward, Arnold used to tell the story to his children, and added, "I never felt so much ashamed in my life--that look and that speech I have never forgotten."

From the numerous instances already cited of men of humble station who have risen to distinction in science and literature, it will be obvious that labor is by no means incompatible with the highest intellectual culture. Work in moderation is healthy as well as agreeable to the human constitution. Work educates the body, as study educates the mind; and that is the best state of society in which there is some work for every man's leisure, and some leisure for every man's work. Even the leisure classes are in a measure compelled to work, sometimes as a relief from *ennui*, but in most cases to gratify and instinct which they cannot resist. Some go foxhunting in the English counties, others grouse shooting on the Scotch hills, while many wander away every summer to climb mountains in Switzerland. Hence the boating, running, cricketing, and athletic sports of the public schools in which our young men at the same time so healthfully cultivate their strength both of mind and body. It is said that the Duke of Wellington, when once looking on at the boys engaged in their sports in the playground at Eton, where he had spent many of his own younger days, made the remark, "It was there that the battle of Waterloo was won!"

Daniel Malthus urged his son when at college to be most diligent in the cultivation of knowledge, but he also enjoined him to pursue manly sports as the best means of keeping up the full working power of his mind, as well as of enjoying the pleasures of intellect. "Every kind of knowledge," said he, "every acquaintance with nature and art, will amuse and strengthen your mind, and I am perfectly pleased that cricket should do the same by your arms and legs; I love to see you excel in exercises of the body, and I think myself that the better half, and so much the most agreeable part, of the pleasures of the mind is best enjoyed while one is upon one's legs." But a still more important use of active employment is that referred to by the great divine, Jeremy Taylor. "Avoid idleness," he says, "and fill up all the spaces of they time with severe and useful employment; for lust easily creeps in at those emptinesses where the soul is unemployed and the body is at ease; for no easy, healthful, idle person was ever chaste, if he could be tempted; but of all employments bodily labor is the most useful, and of the greatest benefit for driving away the devil."

Practical success in life depends more upon physical health than is generally imagined. Hodson, of Hodson's Horse, writing home to a friend in England, said, "I believe if I get on well in India, it will be owing, physically speaking, to a sound digestion." The capacity for continuous working in any calling must necessarily depend in a great measure upon this; and hence the necessity for attending to health, even as a means of intellectual labor. It is perhaps to the neglect of physical exercise that we find amongst students so frequent a tendency toward discontent, unhappiness, inaction, and reverie--displaying itself in contempt for real life and disgust at the beaten tracks of men--a tendency which in England has been called Byronism, and in Germany Wertherism. Dr. Channing noted the same growth in our land, which led him to make the remark, that "too many of our young men grow up in a school of despair." The only remedy for this green-sickness in youth is physical exercise-- action, work and bodily occupation.

The use of early labor in self-imposed mechanical employments may be illustrated by the boyhood of Sir Isaac Newton. Though comparatively a dull scholar, he was very assiduous in the use of his saw, hammer, and hatchet--"knocking and hammering in his lodging room"--making models of windmills, carriages, and machines of all sorts; and as he grew older, he took delight in making little tables and cupboards for his friends. Smeaton, Watt, and Stephenson were equally handy with tools when mere boys; and but for such kind of self-culture in their youth it is doubtful whether they would have accomplished so much in their manhood. Such was also the early training of the great inventors and mechanics described in the preceding pages, whose contrivance and intelligence were practically trained by the constant use of their hands in early life. Even where men belonging to the manual labor class have risen above it, and become more purely intellectual laborers, they have found the advantages of their early training in their later pursuits. Elihu Burritt says he found hard labor *necessary* to enable him to study with effect; and more than once he gave up school teaching and study, and taking to his leather apron again, went back to his blacksmith's forge and anvil for the health of his body and mind's sake.

The training of young men in the use of tools would at the same time that it educated them in "common things," teach them the use of their hands and arms, familiarize them with healthy work, exercise their faculties upon things tangible and actual, give them some practical acquaintance with mechanics, impart to them the ability of being useful, and implant in them the habit of persevering physical effort. This is an advantage which the working classes, strictly so called, certainly possess over the leisure classes--that they are in early life under the necessity of applying themselves laboriously to some mechanical pursuit or other--thus acquiring manual dexterity, and the use of their physical powers. The chief disadvantage attached to the calling of the laborious classes is, not that they are employed in physical work, but that they are too exclusively so employed, often to the neglect of their moral and intellectual faculties. While the youths of the leisure classes, having been taught to associate labor with servility, have shunned it, and been allowed to grow up practically ignorant, the poorer classes, confining themselves within the circle of their laborious callings, have been allowed to grow up, in a large proportion of cases, absolutely illiterate. It seems, possible, however, to avoid both these evils by combining physical training or physical work with intellectual culture; and there are various signs abroad which seem to mark the gradual adoption of this healthier system of education.

The success of even professional men depends in no slight degree on their physical health; and a public writer has gone so far as to say that "the greatness of our great men is quite as much a bodily affair as a mental one." A healthy breathing apparatus is as indispensable to the successful lawyer or politician as a well-cultured intellect. The thorough aeration of his blood by free exposure to a large breathing surface in the lungs is necessary to maintain that vital power on which the vigorous working of the brain in so large a measure depends. The lawyer has to climb the heights of his profession through close and heated courts, and the political leader has to bear the fatigue and excitement of long and anxious debates in a crowded House. Hence the lawyer in full practice and the parliamentary leader in full work are called upon to display powers of physical endurance and activity even more extraordinary than those of the intellect--such powers as have been exhibited in so remarkable a degree by Brougham, Lyndhurst and Campbell; by Peel, Graham and Palmerston--all full-chested men.

Though Sir Walter Scott, when at Edinburgh College, went by the name of "The Greek Blockhead," he was, notwithstanding his lameness, a remarkably healthy youth; he could spear a salmon with the best fisher on the Tweed, and ride a wild horse with any hunter in Yarrow. When devoting himself in after life to literary pursuits, Sir Walter never lost his taste for field sports, but while writing "Waverley" in the morning he would in the afternoon course hares. Professor Wilson was a very athlete, as great at throwing the hammer as in his flights of eloquence and poetry; and Burns, when a youth, was remarkable chiefly for his leaping, putting, and wrestling. Some of the greatest divines were distinguished in their youth for their physical energies. Isaac Barrow, when at the Charterhouse School, was notorious for his pugilistic encounters, in which he got many a bloody nose; Andrew Fuller, when working as a farmer's lad at Soham, was chiefly famous for his skill in boxing; and Adam Clarke, when a boy, was only remarkable for the strength displayed by him in "rolling large stones about"--the secret, possibly, of some of the power which he subsequently displayed in rolling forth large thoughts in his manhood.

While it is necessary, then, in the first place to secure this solid foundation of physical health, it must also be observed that the cultivation of the habit of mental application is quite indispensable for the education of the student. The maxim that "labor conquers all things" holds especially true in the case of the conquest of knowledge. The road into learning is alike free to all who will give the labor and the study requisite to gather it; nor are there any difficulties so great that the student of resolute purpose may not surmount and overcome them. It was one of the characteristic expressions of Chatterton, that God had sent his creatures into the world with arms long enough to reach anything if they chose to be at the trouble. In study, as in business, energy is the great thing. There must be "fervet opus;" we must not only strike the iron while it is hot, but strike it till it is made hot. It is astonishing how much may be accomplished in self-culture by the energetic and the persevering, who are careful to avail themselves of opportunities, and use up the fragments of spare time which the idle permit to run to waste. Thus Ferguson learnt astronomy from the heavens while wrapped in a sheepskin on the highland hills. Thus Stone learnt mathematics while working as a journeyman gardener; thus Drew studied the highest philosophy in the intervals of cobbling shoes; and thus Miller taught himself geology while working as a day laborer in a quarry.

Sir Joshua Reynolds, as we have already observed, was so earnest a believer in the force of industry that he held that all men might achieve excellence if they would but exercise the power of assiduous and patient working. He held that drudgery lay on the road to genius, and that there was no limit to the proficiency of an artist except the limit of his own painstaking. He would not believe in what is called inspiration, but only in study and labor. "Excellence," he said, "is never granted to man but as the reward of labor. If you have great talents, industry will improve them; if you have but moderate abilities, industry will supply their deficiency. Nothing is denied to well-directed labor; nothing is to be obtained without it." Sir Fowell Buxton was an equal believer in the power of study; and he entertained the modest idea that he could do as well as other men if he devoted to the pursuit double the time and labor that they did. He placed his great confidence in ordinary means and extraordinary application.

"I have known several men in my life," says Dr. Ross, "who may be recognized in days to come as men of genius, and they were all plodders, hard-working *intent* men. Genius is known by its works; genius without works is a blind faith, a dumb oracle. But meritorious works are the result of time and labor, and cannot be accomplished by intention or by a wish . . . Every great work is the result of vast preparatory training. Facility comes by labor. Nothing seems easy, not even walking, that was not difficult at first. The orator whose eye flashes instantaneous fire, and whose lips pour out a flood of noble thoughts, startling by their unexpectedness and elevating by their wisdom and truth, has learned his secret by patient repetition, and after many bitter disappointments."

Thoroughness and accuracy are two principal points to be aimed at in study. Francis Horner, in laying down rules for the cultivation of his mind, placed great stress upon the habit of continuous application to one subject for the sake of mastering it thoroughly; he confined himself with this object to only a few books, and resisted with the greatest firmness "every approach to a habit of desultory reading." The value of knowledge to any man consists, not in its quantity, but mainly in the good uses to which he can apply it. Hence a little knowledge of an exact and perfect character is always found more valuable for practical purposes than any extent of superficial learning.

It is not the quantity of study that one gets through, or the amount of reading, that makes a wise man; but the appositeness of the study to the purpose for which it is pursued; the concentration of the mind, for the time being, on the subject under consideration; and the habitual discipline by which the whole system of mental application is regulated. Abernethy was even of opinion that there was a point of saturation in his own mind, and that if he took into it something more than it could hold, it only had the effect of pushing something else out. Speaking of the study of medicine, he said: "If a man has a clear idea of what he desires to do, he will seldom fail in selecting the proper means of accomplishing it."

The most profitable study is that which is conducted with a definite aim and object. By thoroughly mastering any given branch of knowledge we render it more available for use at any moment. Hence it is not enough merely to have books, or to know where to read for information as we want it. Practical wisdom, for the purposes of life, must be carried about with us, and be ready for use at call. It is not sufficient that we have a fund laid up at home, but not a farthing in the pocket: we must carry about with us a store of the current coin of knowledge ready for exchange on all occasions, else we are comparatively helpless when the opportunity for using it occurs.

Decision and promptitude are as requisite in self-culture as in business. The growth of these qualities may be encouraged by accustoming young people to rely upon their own resources, leaving them to enjoy as much freedom of action in early life as is practicable. Too much guidance and restraint hinder the formation of habits of self-help. They are like bladders tied under the arms of one who has not taught himself to swim. Want of confidence is perhaps a greater obstacle to improvement than is generally imagined. It has been said that half the failures in life arise from pulling in one's horse while he is leaping. Dr. Johnson was accustomed to attribute his success to confidence in his own powers. True modesty is quite compatible with a true estimate of one's own merits, and does not demand the abnegation of all merit. Though there are those who deceive themselves by putting a false figure before their ciphers, the want of confidence, the want of faith in one's self, and consequently the want of promptitude in action, is a defect of character which is found to stand very much in the way of individual progress; and the reason why so little is done, is generally because so little is attempted.

There is usually no want of desire on the part of most persons to arrive at the results of self-culture, but there is a great aversion to pay the inevitable price for it, of hard work. Dr. Johnson held that "impatience of study was the mental disease of the present generation;" and the remark is still applicable. We may not believe that there is a royal road to learning, but we seem to believe very firmly in the "popular" one. In education, we invent labor-saving processes, seek short cuts to science, learn French and Latin "in twelve lessons," or "without a master." We resemble the lady of fashion, who engaged a master to teach her on condition that he did not plague her with verbs and participles. We get our smattering of science in the same way; we learn chemistry by listening to a short course of lectures enlivened by experiments, and when we have inhaled laughing-gas, seen green water turned to red, and phosphorus burnt in oxygen, we have got our smattering, of which the most that can be said is, that though it may be better than nothing, it is yet good for nothing. Thus we often imagine we are being educated while we are only being amused.

The facility with which young people are thus induced to acquire knowledge, without study and labor, is not education. It occupies but does not enrich the mind. It imparts a stimulus for the time, and produces a sort of intellectual keenness and cleverness; but, without an implanted purpose and a higher object that mere pleasure, it will bring with it no solid advantage. In such cases knowledge produces but a passing impression; a sensation, gut no more; it is, in fact, the merest epicurism of intelligence--sensuous, but certainly not intellectual. Thus the best qualities of many minds, those which are evoked by vigorous effort and independent action, sleep a deep sleep, and are often never called to life, except by the rough awakening of sudden calamity or suffering, which, in such cases comes as a blessing, if it serves to rouse up a courageous spirit that, but for it, would have slept on.

Accustomed to acquire information under the guise of amusement, young people will soon reject that which is presented to them under the aspect of study and labor. Learning their knowledge and science in sport, they will be too apt to make sport of both; while the habit of intellectual dissipation, thus engendered, cannot fail, in course of time, to produce a thoroughly emasculating effect both upon their mind and character. "Multifarious reading," said Robertson, of Brighton, "weakens the mind like smoking, and is an excuse for its lying dormant. It is the idlest of all idlenesses, and leaves more of impotency than any other."

The evil is a growing one, and operates in various ways. Its least mischief is shallowness; its greatest, the aversion to steady labor which it induces, and the low and feeble tone of mind which it encourages. If we would be really wise, we must diligently apply ourselves, and confront the same continuous application which our forefathers did; for labor is still, and ever will be, the inevitable price set upon everything which is valuable. We must be satisfied to work with a purpose, and wait the results with patience. All progress, of the best kind, is slow; but to him who works faithfully and zealously the reward will, doubtless, be vouchsafed in good time. The spirit of industry, embodies in a man's daily life, will gradually lead him to exercise his powers on objects outside himself, of greater dignity and more extended usefulness. And still we must labor on; for the work of self-culture is never finished. "To be employed," said the poet Gray, "is to be happy." "It is better to wear out that rust out," said Bishop Cumberland. "Have we not all eternity to rest in?" exclaimed Arnauld. "Repos ailleurs" (rest for others) was the motto of Marnix de St. Aldegonde, the energetic and ever-working friend of William the Silent.

It is the use we make of the powers entrusted to us which constitutes our only just claims to respect. He who employs his one talent aright is as much to be honored as he to whom ten talents have been given. There is really no more personal merit attaching to the possession of superior intellectual powers than there is in the succession to a large estate. How are those powers used--how is that estate employed? The mind may accumulate large stores of knowledge without any useful purpose; but the knowledge must be allied to goodness and wisdom, and embodied in upright character, else it is naught. Pestalozzi even held intellectual training by itself to be pernicious; insisting that the roots of all knowledge must strike and feed in the soil of the rightly-governed will. The acquisition of knowledge may, it is true, protect a man against the meaner felonies of life; but not in any degree against its selfish vices, unless fortified by sound principles and habits. Hence do we find in daily life so many instances of men who are well-informed in intellect, but utterly deformed in character; filled with the learning of the schools, yet possessing little practical wisdom, and offering examples for warning rather than imitation. An often-quoted expression at this day is that "Knowledge is power;" but also, are fanaticism, despotism, and ambition. Knowledge of itself, unless wisely directed might merely make bad men more dangerous, and the society in which it was regarded as the highest good, as little better than pandemonium.

It is not then how much a man may know, that is of importance, but the end and purpose for which he knows it. The object of knowledge should be to mature wisdom and improve character, to render us better, happier, and more useful; more benevolent, more energetic, and more efficient in the pursuit of every high purpose in life. "When people once fall into the habit of admiring and encouraging ability as such, without reference to moral character--and religious and political opinions are the concrete form of moral character--they are on the highway to all sorts of degradation." We must ourselves *be* and *do*, and not rest satisfied merely with reading and meditating over what other men have been and done. Our best light must be made life, and our best thought action. At least we ought to be able to say, as Richter did, "I have made as much out of myself as could be made of the stuff, and no man should require more;" for it is every man's duty to discipline and guide himself, with God's help, according to his responsibilities and the faculties with which he has been endowed.

Self-discipline and self-control are the beginnings of practical wisdom; and these must have their root in self-respect. Hope springs from it--hope, which is the companion of power, and the mother of success; for whoso hopes strongly has within him the gift of miracles. The humblest may say, "To respect myself, to develop myself--this is my true duty in life. An integral and responsible part of the great system of society, I owe it to society and to its Author not to degrade of destroy either my body, mind, or instincts. On the contrary, I am bound to the best of my power to give to those parts of my constitution the highest degree of perfection possible. I am not only to suppress the evil, but to evoke the good elements in my nature. And as I respect myself, so am I equally bound to respect others, as they on their part are bound to respect me." Hence mutual respect, justice, and order, of which law becomes the written record and guarantee.

Self-respect is the noblest garment with which a man may clothe himself--the most elevating feeling with which the mind can be inspired. One of Pythagoras' wisest maxims, in his "Golden Verses," is that with which he enjoins the pupil to "reverence himself." Borne up by this high idea, he will not defile his body by sensuality, nor his mind by servile thoughts. This sentiment, carried into daily life, will be found at the root of all the virtues--cleanliness, sobriety, chastity, morality, and religion. "The pious and just honoring of ourselves," said Milton, "may be thought the radical moisture and fountain-head from whence every laudable and worthy enterprise issues forth." To think meanly of one's self, is to sink in one's own estimation as well as in the estimation of others. And as the thoughts are, so will the acts be. Man cannot aspire if he looks down; if he will rise, he must look up. The very humblest may be sustained by the proper indulgence of this feeling. Poverty itself may be lifted and lighted up by self-respect; and it is truly a noble sight to see a poor man hold himself upright amidst his temptations, and refuse to demean himself by low actions.

CHAPTER XXIII
LABOR CREATES THE ONLY TRUE NOBILITY.

As Americans we are justly proud that we have no hereditary titles, but each man is measured by his own personal worth.

While believing firmly in the propriety of this order of things, yet we would not have you imagine that we underestimate the value of a respectable lineage, but it is better to be the originator of a great family than to be the degenerate descendant of one.

With but few exceptions those Americans whose lives are very properly held up as an example for the imitation of our youth, are men who have had to work their own way from the humblest walks in life, to the highest in the gift of the nation.

This is true of Franklin, the statesman and philosopher, as it is of Lincoln, the patriot and martyr, and the splendid list of names that adorn the pages of our intervening history.

Smiles in his "Self-Help" shows how in England, a land where ancestry counts for so much, the descendants of the greatest men, even of kings, have been found in the humblest of callings.

The blood of all men flows from equally remote sources; and though some are unable to trace their line directly beyond their grandfathers, all are nevertheless justified in placing at the head of their pedigree the great progenitors of the race, as Lord Chesterfield did when he wrote, "ADAM *de Stanhope*--EVE *de Stanhope*." No class is ever long stationary. The mighty fall, and the humble are exalted. New families take the place of the old, who disappear among the ranks of the common people. Burke's "Vicissitudes of Families" strikingly exhibits the rise and fall of families, and shows that the misfortunes which overtake the rich and noble are greater in proportion than those which overwhelm the poor. This author points out that of the twenty-five barons selected to enforce the observance of Magna Charta, there is not now in the House of Peers a single male descendant. Civil wars and rebellions ruined many of the old nobility and dispersed their families. Yet their descendants in many cases survive, and are to be found among the ranks of the people. Fuller wrote in his "Worthies," that "some who justly hold the surnames of Bohuns, Mortimers, and Plantagenets, are hid in the heap of common men." Thus Burke shows that two of the lineal descendants of the Earl of Kent, sixth son of Edward I, were discovered in a butcher and a toll-gatherer; that the great-grandson of Margaret Plantagenet, daughter of the Duke of Clarence, sank to the condition of a cobbler at Newport, in Shropshire; and that among the lineal descendants of the Duke of Gloucester, son of Edward III, was the late sexton of St. George's Church, London. It is understood that the lineal descendant of Simon de Montfort, England's premier baron, is a saddler in Tooley street. One of the descendants of the "Proud Percys," a claimant of the title of Duke of Northumberland, was a Dublin trunkmaker; and not many years since one of the claimants for the title of Earl of Perth presented himself in the person of a laborer in a Northumberland coal-pit. Hugh Miller, when working as a stone-mason near Edinburgh, was served by a hodman, who was one of the numerous claimants for the earldom of Crauford--all that was wanted to establish his claim being a missing marriage certificate; and while the work was going on, the cry resounded from the walls many times in the day, of "John, Yearl Crauford, bring us another hod o' lime." One of Oliver Cromwell's great-grandsons was a grocer in London, and others of his descendants died in great poverty. Many barons of proud names and titles have perished, like the sloth, upon their family tree, after eating up all the leaves; while others have been overtaken by adversities which they have been unable to retrieve, and have sunk at last into poverty and obscurity. Such are the mutabilities of rank and fortune.

The great bulk of the English peerage is comparatively modern, so far as the titles go; but it is not the less noble that it has been recruited to so large an extent from the ranks of honorable industry. In olden times, the wealth and commerce of London, conducted as it was by energetic and enterprising men, was a prolific source of peerages. Thus, the earldom of Cornwallis was founded by Thomas Cornwallis, the Cheapside merchant; that of Essex by William Capel, the draper;

and that of Craven by William Craven, the merchant tailor. The modern Earl of Warwick is not descended from the "King- maker," but from William Greville, the woolstapler; whilst the modern dukes of Northumberland find their head, not in the Percys, but in Hugh Smithson, a respectable London apothecary. The founders of the families of Dartmouth, Radnor, Ducie, and Pomfret, were respectively a skinner, a silk manufacturer, a merchant tailor, and a Calais merchant; whilst the founders of the peerages of Tankerville, Dormer, and Coventry, were mercers. The ancestors of Earl Romney, and Lord Dudley and Ward, were goldsmiths and jewelers; and Lord Dacres was a banker in the reign of Charles I, as Lord Overstone is in that of Queen Victoria. Edward Osborne, the founder of the dukedom of Leeds, was apprentice to William Hewet, a rich cloth-worker on London Bridge, whose only daughter he courageously rescued from drowning, by leaping into the Thames after her, and whom he eventually married.

William Phipps, at one time Colonial Governor of Massachusetts, and the founder of the Normandy family, was the son of a gunsmith who emigrated to Maine, where this remarkable man was born in 1651. He was one of a family of not fewer than twenty-six children (of whom twenty-one were sons), whose only fortune lay in their stout hearts and strong arms. William seems to have had a sash of the Danish seablood in his veins, and he did not take kindly to the quiet life of a shepherd in which he spent his early years. By nature bold and adventurous, he longed to become a sailor and roam through the world. He sought to join some ship; but not being able to find one, he apprenticed himself to a ship-builder, with whom he thoroughly learnt his trade, acquiring the arts of reading and writing during his leisure hours. Having completed his apprenticeship and removed to Boston, he wooed and married a widow of some means, after which he set up a little ship-building yard of his own, built a ship, and putting to sea in her, he engaged in the lumber trade, which he carried on in a plodding and laborious way for the space of about ten years.

It happened that one day, while passing through the crooked streets of old Boston, he overheard some sailors talking to each other of a wreck which had just taken place off the Bahamas; that of a Spanish ship, supposed to have much money on board. His adventurous spirit was at once kindled, and getting together a likely crew without loss of time, he set sail for the Bahamas. The wreck being well in shore he easily found it, and succeeded in recovering a great deal of its cargo, but very little money; and the result was that he barely defrayed his expenses. His success had been such, however, as to stimulate his enterprising spirit; and when he was told of another and far more richly laden vessel which had been wrecked near Port de la Plata more than half a century before, he forthwith formed the resolution of raising the wreck, or at all events of fishing up the treasure.

Being too poor, however, to undertake such an enterprise without powerful help, he set sail for England in the hope that he might there obtain it. The fame of his success in raising the wreck off the Bahamas had already preceded him. He applied direct to the Government. By his urgent enthusiasm, he succeeded in overcoming the usual inertia of official minds; and Charles II eventually placed at his disposal the "Rose Algier," a ship of eighteen guns and ninety- five men, appointing him to the chief command.

Phipps then set sail to find the Spanish ship and fish up the treasure. He reached the coast of Hispaniola in safety; but how to find the sunken ship was the great difficulty. The fact of the wreck was more than fifty years old; and Phipps had only the traditionary rumors of the even to work upon. There was a wide coast to explore, and an outspread ocean, without any trace whatever of the argosy which lay somewhere at its bottom. But the man was stout in heart and full of hope. He set his seamen to work to drag along the coast, and for weeks they went on fishing up seaweed, shingle and bits of rock. No occupation could be more trying to seamen, and they began to grumble one to another, and to whisper that the man in command had brought them on a fool's errand.

At length the murmurers gained head, and the men broke into open mutiny. A body of them rushed one day on to the quarter-deck, and demanded that the voyage should be relinquished. Phipps, however, was not a man to be intimidated; he seized the ringleaders, and sent the others back to their duty. It became necessary to bring the ship to anchor close to a small island for the purpose of repairs; and, to lighten her, the chief part of the stores was landed. Discontent still increasing among the crew, a new plot was laid among the men on shore to seize the ship, throw Phipps overboard, and start on a piratical cruise against the Spaniards in the South Seas. But it was necessary to secure the services of the chief ship-carpenter, who was consequently made privy to the plot. This man proved faithful, and a once told the captain of his danger. Summoning about him those whom he knew to be loyal, Phipps had the ship's guns loaded, which commanded the shore, and ordered the bridge communicating with the vessel to be drawn up. When the mutineers made their appearance, the captain hailed them, and told the men he would fire upon them if they approached the stores (still on land), when they drew back; on which Phipps had the stores reshipped under cover of his guns. The mutineers, fearful of being left upon the barren island, threw down their arms and implored to be permitted to return to their duty. The request was granted, and suitable precautions were taken against further mischief. Phipps, however, took the first opportunity of landing the mutinous part of the crew, and engaging other men in their places; but, by the time that he could again proceed actively with his explorations, he found it absolutely necessary to proceed to England for the purpose of repairing the ship. He had now, however, gained more precise information as to the spot where the Spanish treasure-ship had sunk; and, though as yet baffled, he was more confident than ever of the eventual success of his enterprise.

Returned to London, Phipps reported the result of his voyage to the Admirality, who professed to be pleased with his exertions; but he had been unsuccessful, and they would not entrust him with another king's ship. James II was now on the throne, and the Government was in trouble; so Phipps and his golden project appealed to them in vain. He next tried to raise the requisite means by a public subscription. At first he was laughed at; but his ceaseless importunity at length prevailed, and after four years' dinning of his project into the ears of the great and influential--during which time he lived in poverty--he at length succeeded. A company was formed in twenty shares, The Duke of Albemarle, son of General Monk, taking the chief interest in it, and subscribing the principal part of the necessary fund for the prosecution of the enterprise.

Phipps was successful in this undertaking. He started other enterprises and succeeded. He was knighted, and as has been stated, became the founder of one of England's noble families. It should be said, however, that beyond his perseverance, he had but few qualities to commend him. He was coarse, ignorant, and brutal, and had to fly from Massachusetts to save his life from an indignant people.

But true nobility is not that which is conferred by the warrant of a monarch. If as Pope says, "An honest man's the noblest work of God," then the nobles man is the honest man, who with his own clear brain and strong right arm, wins his way up from the humblest walks in life, till by virtue of his manhood, he stands the peer of peers, and by Divine right the equal of all earth's kings.

We hear a great deal about an American aristocracy, but no matter what the wishes of a few people with un-American tastes may be, the only aristocracy that can ever find recognition here, is that of brains and the success born of hones toil.

Ninety-nine out of every hundred of the rich families that are wrongly supposed to constitute our aristocracy at this time, were poor less than fifty years ago. Many of the rich families of fifty years ago are poor to-day; and so fortune varies and changes in this new land. Our true aristocrats are successful men like Peter Cooper, who left the world better for having lived in it. We count among our aristocrats, patriots like Lincoln, and if his descendants emulate his noble example, they too will be ennobled by their countrymen. We reckon Lowell, Longfellow, Whittier, Holmes, Hawthorne, Elisha Howe and George W. Childs among our aristocrats. Andrew Carnegie deserves a place in the same list of American peers, as does Thomas A. Edison.

But after all the true title to nobility is implied in the words "gentleman" and "lady," and with these we need not fear comparison with all the world's titled nobles.

CHAPTER XXIV
THE SUCCESSFUL MAN IS SELF-MADE.

The crown and glory of life is Character. It is the noblest possession of a man, constituting a rank in itself, and an estate in the general good-will; dignifying every station, and exalting every position in society. It exercises a greater power than wealth, and secures all the honor without the jealousies of fame. It carries with it an influence which always tells; for it is the result of proved honor, rectitude and consistency--qualities which, perhaps, more than any other, command the general confidence and respect of mankind.

Character is human nature in its best form It is moral order embodied in the individual. Men of character are not only the conscience of society, but in every well-governed state they are its best motive power; for it is moral qualities in the main which rule the world. Even in war, Napoleon said, the moral is to the physical as ten to one. The strength, the industry, and the civilization of nations--all depend upon individual character; and the very foundations of civil security rest upon it. Laws and institutions are but its outgrowth. In the just balance of nature individuals, nations and races, will obtain just so much as they deserve, and no more. And as effect finds its cause, so surely does quality of character amongst a people produce its befitting results.

Though a man have comparatively little culture, slender abilities, and but small wealth, yet, if his character be of sterling worth, he always commands an influence, whether it be in the workshop, the counting-house, the mart, or the senate. Canning wisely wrote in 1801, "My road must be through Character to Power; I will try no other course; and I am sanguine enough to believe that this course, though not perhaps the quickest, is the surest." You may admire men of intellect; but something more is necessary before you will trust them. This was strikingly il-

lustrated in the career of Francis Horner--a man of whom Sydney Smith said that
the Ten Commandments were stamped upon his countenance. "The valuable and
peculiar light," says Lord Cockburn, "in which his history is calculated to inspire
every right-minded youth, is this: He died at the age of thirty- eight; possessed of
greater public influence than any other private man, and admired, beloved, trusted,
and deplored by all, except the heartless or the base. Now let every young man ask-
-how was this attained? By rank? He was the son of an Edinburgh merchant. By
wealth? Neither he, nor any of his relations, ever had a superfluous sixpence. By office? He held but one, and only for a few years, of no influence, and with very little
pay. By talents? His were not splendid, and he had no genius. Cautious and slow, his
only ambition was to be right. By eloquence? He spoke in calm, good taste, without
any of the oratory that either terrifies or seduces. By any fascination of manner? His
was only correct and agreeable. By what, then, was it? Merely by sense, industry,
good principles, and a good heart--qualities which no well-constituted mind need
ever despair of attaining. It was the force of his character that raised him; and this
character not impressed upon him by nature, but formed, out of no peculiarly fine
elements, by himself. There were many in the House of Commons of far greater
ability and eloquence. But no one surpassed him in the combination of an adequate
portion of these with moral worth. Horner was born to show what moderate powers, unaided by anything whatever except culture and goodness, may achieve, even
when these powers are displayed amidst the competition and jealousy of public
life."

Franklin attributed his success as a public man not to his talents or his powers
of speaking--for these were but moderate--but to his known integrity of character. Hence, it was, he says, "that I had so much weight with my fellow-citizens. I
was but a bad speaker, never eloquent, subject to much hesitation in my choice of
words, hardly correct in language, and yet I generally carried my point." Character
creates confidence in men in high station as well as in humble life. It was said of the
first Emperor Alexander of Russia, that his personal character was equivalent to a
constitution. During the wars of the Fronde, Montaigne was the only man amongst
the French gentry who kept his castle gates unbarred; and it was said of him, that
his personal character was a better protection for him than a regiment of horse
would have been.

That character is power, is true in a much higher sense than that knowledge is power. Mind without heart, intelligence without conduct, cleverness without goodness, are powers in their way, but they may be powers only for mischief. We may be instructed or amused by them; but it is sometimes as difficult to admire them as it would be to admire the dexterity of a pickpocket or the horsemanship of a highwayman.

Truthfulness, integrity, and goodness--qualities that hang not on any man's breath--form the essence of manly character, or, as one of our old writers has it, "that inbred loyalty unto Virtue which can serve her without a livery." He who possesses these qualities, united with strength of purpose, carries with him a power which is irresistible. He is strong to do good, strong to resist evil, and strong to bear up under difficulty and misfortune. When Stephen of Colonna fell into the hands of his base assailants, and they asked him in derision, "Where is now your fortress?" "Here," was his bold reply, placing his hand upon his heart. It is in misfortune that the character of the upright man shines forth with the greatest lustre; and when all else fails, he takes his stand upon his integrity and his courage.

The rules of conduct followed by Lord Erskine--a man of sterling independence of principle and scrupulous adherence to truth--are worthy of being engraven on every young man's heart. "It was a first command and counsel of my earliest youth," he said, "always to do what my conscience told me to be a duty, and to leave the consequence to God. I shall carry with me the memory, and I trust the practice, of this parental lesson to the grave. I have hitherto followed it, and I have no reason to complain that my obedience to it has been a temporal sacrifice. I have found it, on the contrary, the road to prosperity and wealth, and I shall point out the same path to my children for their pursuit."

Every man is bound to aim at the possession of a good character as one of the highest objects of life. The very effort to secure it by worthy means will furnish him with a motive of exertion; and his idea of manhood, in proportion as it is elevated, will steady and animate his motive. It is well to have a high standard of life, even though we may not be able altogether to realize it. "The youth," says Mr. Disraeli, "who does not look up will look down; and the spirit that does not soar is destined perhaps to grovel." George Herbert wisely writes:

"Pitch thy behavior low, thy projects high, So shall thou humble and magnanimous be. Sink not in spirit; who aimeth at the sky Shoots higher much that he that means a tree."

He who has a high standard of living and thinking will certainly do better than he who has none at all. "Pluck at a gown of gold," says the Scotch proverb, "and you may get a sleeve o't." Whoever tries for the highest results cannot fail to reach a point far in advance of that from which he started; and though the end attained may fall short of that proposed, still, the very effort to rise, of itself cannot fail to prove permanently beneficial.

There are many counterfeits of character, but the genuine article is difficult to be mistaken. Some, knowing its money value, would assume its disguise for the purpose of imposing upon the unwary. Colonel Charteris said to a man distinguished for his honesty, "I would give a thousand pounds for your good name." "Why?" "Because I could make ten thousand by it," was the knave's reply.

There is a truthfulness in action as well as in words, which is essential to uprightness of character. A man must really be what he seems or purposes to be. When an American gentleman wrote to Granville Sharp, that from respect for his great virtues he had named one of his sons after him, Sharp replied: "I must request you to teach him a favorite maxim of the family whose name you have given him—*Always endeavor to be really what you would wish to appear*. This maxim, as my father informed me, was carefully and humbly practiced by *his* father, whose sincerity, as a plain and honest man, thereby became the principal feature of his character, both in public and private life." Every man who respects himself, and values the respect of others, will carry out the maxim in act—doing honestly what he purposes to do—putting the highest character into his work, scrimping nothing, but priding himself upon his integrity and conscientiousness. Once Cromwell said to Bernard—a clever but somewhat unscrupulous lawyer, "I understand that you have lately been vastly wary in your conduct; do not be too confident of this: subtlety may deceive you, integrity never will." Men whose acts are at direct variance with their words, command no respect, and what they say has but little weight: even truths, when uttered by them, seem to come blasted from their lips.

The true character acts rightly, whether in secret or in the sight of men. That boy was well trained who, when asked why he did not pocket some pears, for nobody was there to see, replied, "Yes, there was; I was there to see myself; and I don't intend ever to see myself do a dishonest thing." This is a simple but not inappropriate illustration of principle, or conscience, dominating in the character, and exercising a noble protectorate over it; not merely a passive influence, but an active power regulating the life. Such a principle goes on moulding the character hourly and daily, growing with a force that operates every moment. Without this dominating influence, character has no protection, but is constantly liable to fall away before temptation; and every such temptation succumbed to, every act of meanness or dishonesty, however slight, causes self-degradation. It matters not whether the act be successful or not, discovered or concealed; the culprit is no longer the same, but another person; and he is pursued by a secret uneasiness, by self-reproach, or the workings of what we call conscience, which is the inevitable doom of the guilty.

And here it may be observed how greatly the character may be strengthened and supported by the cultivation of good habits. Man, it has been said, is a bundle of habits; and habit is second nature. Metastasio entertained so strong an opinion as to the power of repetition in act and thought, that he said, "All is habit in mankind, even virtue itself." Butler, in his "Analogy," impresses the importance of careful self-discipline and firm resistance to temptation, as tending to make virtue habitual, so that at length it may become more easy to do good than to give way to sin. "As habits belonging to the body," he says, "are produced by external acts, so habits of the mind are produced by the execution of inward practical purposes, i.e., carrying them into act, or acting upon them--the principles of obedience, veracity, justice, and charity." And again, Lord Brougham says, when enforcing the immense importance of training and example in youth, "I trust everything, under God, to habit, on which, in all ages, the lawgiver, as well as the schoolmaster, has mainly placed his reliance; habit, which makes everything easy, and cast the difficulties upon the deviation from a wonted course." Thus, make sobriety a habit and intemperance will be hateful; make prudence a habit, and reckless profligacy will become revolting to every principle of conduct which regulates the life of the individual. Hence the necessity for the greatest care and watchfulness against the inroad of any evil habit; for the character is always weakest at that point at which it has once given way; and it is long before a principle restored can become as firm as one that has never been moved. It is a fine remark of a Russian writer, that "Habits are a necklace of pearls: untie the knot, and the whole unthreads."

Wherever formed, habit acts involuntarily and without effort; and it is only when you oppose it, that you find how powerful it has become. What is done once and again, soon gives facility and proneness. The habit at first may seem to have no more strength than a spider's web; but, once formed, it binds us with a chain of iron. The small events of life, taken singly, may seem exceedingly unimportant, like snow that falls silently, flake by flake; yet accumulated, these snowflakes form the avalanche.

Self-respect, self-help, application, industry, integrity--all are of the nature of habits, not beliefs. Principles, in fact, are but the names which we assign to habits; for the principles are words, but the habits are the things themselves: benefactors or tyrants, according as they are good or evil. It thus happens that as we grow older, a portion of our free activity and individuality becomes suspended in habit; our actions become of the nature of fate; and we are bound by the chains which we have woven around ourselves.

It is indeed scarcely possible to overestimate the importance of training the young to virtuous habits. In them they are the easiest formed, and when formed, they last for life; like letters cut on the bark of a tree, they grow and widen with age. "Train up a child in the way he should go, and when he is old he will not depart from it." The beginning holds within it the end; the first start on the road of life determines the direction and the destination of the journey. Remember, before you are five-and-twenty you must establish a character that will serve you all your life. As habit strengthens with age, and character becomes formed, and turning into a new path becomes more and more difficult. Hence, it is often harder to unlearn that to learn; and for this reason the Grecian flute-player was justified who charged double fees to those pupils who had been taught by an inferior master. To uproot and old habit is sometimes a more painful thing, and vastly more difficult, than to wrench out a tooth. Try and reform an habitually indolent, or improvident, or drunken person, and in a large majority of cases you will fail. For the habit in each case has wound itself in and through life until it has become an integral part of it, and can not be uprooted. Hence, as Mr. Lynch observes, "the wisest habit of all is the habit of care in the formation of good habits."

Even happiness itself may become habitual. There is a habit of looking at the bright side of things, and also of looking at the dark side. Dr. Johnson said that the habit of looking at the best side of a thing is worth more to a man than a thousand pounds a year. And we possess the power, to a great extent, of so exercising the will as to direct the thoughts upon objects calculated to yield happiness and improvement rather than their opposites. In this way the habit of happy thought may be made to spring up like any other habit. And to bring up men or women with a genial nature of this sort, a good temper, and a happy frame of mind is, perhaps, of even more importance, in may cases, than to perfect them in much knowledge and many accomplishments.

As daylight can be seen through very small holes, so little things will illustrate a person's character. Indeed, character consists in little acts, well and honorably performed; daily life being the quarry from which we build it up, and rough-hew the habits which form it. One of the most marked tests of character is the manner in which we conduct ourselves toward others. A graceful behavior toward superiors, inferiors, and equals, is a constant source of pleasure. It pleases others because it indicates respect for their personality; but it gives tenfold more pleasure to ourselves. Every man may, to a large extent, be a self-educator in good behavior, as in everything else; he can be civil and kind, if he will, though he have not a cent in his pocket. Gentleness in society is like the silent influence of light, which gives color to all nature; it is far more powerful than loudness or force, and far more fruitful. It pushes its way quietly and persistently, like the tiniest daffodil in spring, which raises the clod and thrusts it aside by the simple persistency of growing.

Even a kind look will give pleasure and confer happiness. In one of Robertson's letters, he tells of a lady who related to him "the delight, the tears of gratitude, which she had witnessed in a poor girl to whom, in passing I gave a kind look on going out of church on Sunday. What a lesson! How cheaply happiness can be given! What opportunities we miss of doing an angel's work! I remember doing it, full of sad feelings, passing on, and thinking no more about it; and it gave an hour's sunshine to a human life, and lightened the load of life to a human heart for a time."

Morals and manners, which give color to life, are of much greater importance than laws, which are but their manifestations. The law touches us here and there, but manners are about us everywhere, pervading society like the air we breathe. Good manners, as we call them, are neither more nor less than good behavior; consisting of courtesy and kindness; benevolence being the preponderating element in all kinds of mutually beneficial and pleasant intercourse amongst human beings. "Civility," said Lady Montague, "costs nothing and buys everything." The cheapest of all things is kindness, its exercise requiring the least possible trouble and self-sacrifice. "Win hearts," said Burleigh to Queen Elizabeth, "and you have all men's hearts and purses." If we would only let nature act kindly, free from affectation and artifice, the results on social good humor and happiness would be incalculable. The little courtesies which form the small change of life, may separately appear of little intrinsic value, but they acquire their importance from repetition and accumulation. They are like the spare minutes, or the groat a day, which proverbially produce such momentous results in the course of a twelvemonth, or in a lifetime.

Manners are the ornament of action; and there is a way of speaking a kind word, or of doing a kind thing, which greatly enhances its value. What seems to be done with a grudge, or as an act of condescension, is scarcely accepted as a favor. Yet there are men who pride themselves upon their gruffness; and though they may possess virtue and capacity, their manner is often such as to render them almost insupportable. It is difficult to like a man who, though he may not pull your nose, habitually wounds your self-respect, and takes a pride in saying disagreeable things to you. There are others who are dreadfully condescending, and cannot avoid seizing upon every small opportunity of making their greatness felt. When Abernethy was canvassing for the office of surgeon to St. Bartholomew's Hospital, he called upon such a person--a rich grocer, one of the governors. The great man behind the counter seeing the great surgeon enter immediately assumed the grand air toward the supposed suppliant for his vote. "I presume, sir," he said, "you want my vote and interest at this momentous epoch of your life." Abernethy, who hated humbugs, and felt nettled at the tone, replied: "No, I don't; I want a pennyworth of figs; come, look sharp and wrap them up; I want to be off!"

The gentleman is eminently distinguished for his self-respect. He values his character--not so much of it only as can be seen by others, but as he sees himself; having regard for the approval of his inward monitor. And, as he respects himself, so, by the same law, does he respect others. Humanity is sacred in his eyes; and thence proceed politeness and forbearance, kindness and charity. It is related of Lord Edward Fitzgerald that, while traveling in Canada, in company with the Indians, he was shocked by the sight of a poor squaw trudging along laden with her husband's trappings, while the chief himself walked on unencumbered. Lord Edward at once relieved the squaw of her pack by placing it upon his own shoulders--a beautiful instance of what the French call *politesse de coeur*--the inbred politeness of the true gentleman.

The true gentleman has a keen sense of honor--scrupulously avoiding mean actions. His standard of probity in word and action is high. He does not shuffle or prevaricate, dodge or skulk; but is honest, upright and straightforward. His law is rectitude--action in right lines. When he says *yes*, it is a law; and he dares to say the valiant *no* at the fitting season.

Riches and rank have no necessary connection with genuine gentlemanly qualities. The poor man may be a true gentleman--in spirit and in daily life. He may be honest, truthful, upright, polite, temperate, courageous, self-respecting, and self-helping--that is, be a true gentleman. The poor man with a rich spirit is in all ways superior to the rich man with a poor spirit. To borrow S. Paul's words, the former is as "having nothing, yet possessing all things," while the other, though possessing all things, has nothing. The first hopes everything, and fears nothing; the last hopes nothing, and fears everything. Only the poor in spirit are really poor. He who has lost all, but retains his courage, cheerfulness, hope, virtue, and self- respect, is still rich. For such a man, the world is, as it were, held in trust; his spirit dominating over its grosser cares, he can still walk erect, a true gentleman.

Occasionally, the brave and gentle character may be found under the humblest garb. Here is an old illustration, but a fine one. Once on a time, when the Adige suddenly overflowed its banks, the bridge of Verona was carried away with the exception of the centre arch, on which stood a house, whose inhabitants supplicated help from the windows, while the foundations were visibly giving way. "I will give a hundred French louis," said the Count Spolverini, who stood by, "to any person who will venture to deliver those unfortunate people." A young peasant came forth from the crowd, seized a boat, and pushed into the stream. He gained the pier, received the whole family into the boat, and made for the shore, where he landed them in safety. "Here is your money, my brave young fellow," said the count. "No," was the answer of the young man, "I do not sell my life; give the money to this poor family, who have need of it." Here spoke the true spirit of the gentleman, though he was in the garb of a peasant.

There is perhaps no finer example in all history of the self-made man than George Washington. It may be argued that he belonged to a good family, and that his family was amongst the richest in the country at that time. This is true, yet there is not a boy who graduates to-day at our grammar schools who has not had far better educational advantages than had Washington. But he was self-taught, and he so prepared himself that no duty that required him, ever found him deficient. At an age when most young men are thinking about striking out for themselves, Washington occupied with success and honor positions requiring courage, judgment, and decision. He grew with his own deserved advance, until at length by his own splendid efforts, he found himself, in the words of Adams, "First in war, first in peace, and first in the hearts of his countrymen."

With all the avenues of life open to him, or ready to be opened, if he will but boldly knock, the young man starting out in life to-day has every advantage. If he will carefully study over the splendid examples we have cited, and follow along the lines that led to their success, his own prosperity can no longer be a matter for doubt.

CHAPTER XXV
UNSELFISHNESS AND HELPFULNESS.

It must never be forgotten that the position a man occupies at the close of his life is not an infallible criterion of whether he has got on in the world. There are some places in the world's history so illustrious that to occupy them it would be worth dying in poverty and misery. Ambition might well choose to be remembered with gratitude by succeeding generations and to have an immortal name, even if to attain it everything were sacrificed that is counted desirable in life. Who would not surrender wealth and ease and luxury, if in exchange for them he could leave such a name as Columbus, Washington, Lincoln, John Brown, Livingstone or Howard? Posthumous glory counts for something in the reckoning. And this is often attained by self-sacrifice. Revile the world as we may, it does not forget the men who have done it service. The men who have forgotten themselves, who have not striven after their own advantage, but have devoted their lives to the good of humanity, achieve immortality. They get on in the world in the sense of receiving a crown that cannot fade and a glory outshining that of kings and millionaires. The hero has a reward all his own and he may well renounce the lower rewards of riches and ease to gain it. But his qualities must be heroic or he will make his sacrifices to no purpose. He must be true to himself at all cost. Washington was a brilliant example of this fidelity to his ideal. Sparks tells us that when he clearly saw his duty before him, he did it at all hazards, and with inflexible integrity. He did not do it for effect; nor did he think of glory, or of fame and its rewards; but of the right thing to be done, and the best way of doing it.

Yet Washington had a most modest opinion of himself; and when offered the chief command of the American patriot army he hesitated to accept it until it was pressed upon him. When acknowledging in Congress the honor which had been done him in selecting him to so important a trust, on the execution of which the future of his country in a great measure depended, Washington said: "I beg it may be remembered, lest some unlucky event should happen unfavorable to my reputation, that I this day declare, with the utmost sincerity, I do not think myself equal to the command I am honored with."

And in his letter to his wife, communicating to her his appointment as commander-in-chief, he said: "I have used very endeavor in my power to avoid it, not only from my unwillingness to part with you and the family, but from a consciousness of its being a trust too great for my capacity; and that I should enjoy more real happiness in one month with you at home than I have the most distant prospect of finding abroad, if my stay were to be seven times seven years. But, as it has been a kind of destiny that has thrown me upon this service, I shall hope that my undertaking is designed for some good purpose. It was utterly out of my power to refuse the appointment, without exposing my character to such censures as would have reflected dishonor upon myself, and given pain to my friends. This, I am sure, could not, and ought not, to be pleasing to you, and must have lessened me considerably in my own esteem."

Washington pursued his upright course through life, first as commander-in-chief, and afterward as President, never faltering in the path of duty. He had no regard for popularity, but held to his purpose through good and through evil report, often at the risk of his power and influence. Thus, on one occasion, when the ratification of a treaty, arranged by Mr. Jay with Great Britain, was in question, Washington was urged to reject it. But his honor, and the honor of his country, was committed, and he refused to do so. A great outcry was raised against the treaty, and for a time Washington was so unpopular that he is said to have been actually stoned by the mob. But he, nevertheless, held it to be his duty to ratify the treaty; and it was carried out in despite of petitions and remonstrances from all quarters. "While I fell," he said, in answer to the remonstrants, "the most lively gratitude for the many instances of approbation from my country, I can no otherwise deserve it than by obeying the dictates of my conscience."

When the Oregon, coming along the Atlantic coast, was struck in the middle of the night by that coaster, and a great wound was made in her side, through which the water was pouring, Captain Murray stood on the bridge as calm, apparently, as a May morning, and waited until every passenger was off, and every officer was off, and every man on the crew was off, and the last man to step from the sinking ship was the captain himself; and ten minutes after he stepped off, the steamer gave a quiver, as of apprehension, and then plunged to the bottom of the ocean. The steamer was his, and the men were his, and the boats were his, and the passengers were his, all for this: that he might save them in time of peril; and he would go down to the bottom of the ocean rather than that, by his recreancy, one of those entrusted to him should perish. This was the true hero, the man who would die rather than be false to duty.

One of the most striking instances that could be given of the character of the dutiful, truthful, laborious man, who works on bravely in spite of difficulty and physical suffering, is presented in the life of the late George Wilson, Professor of Technology in the University of Edinburgh. Wilson's life was, indeed, a marvel of cheerful laboriousness; exhibiting the power of the soul to triumph over the body, and almost to set it at defiance. It might be taken as an illustration of the saying of the whaling-captain to Dr. Kane, as to the power of moral force over physical: "Bless you, sir, the soul will any day lift the body out of its boots!"

A fragile but bright and lively boy, he had scarcely entered manhood ere his constitution began to exhibit signs of disease. As early, indeed, as his seventeenth year, he began to complain of melancholy and sleeplessness, supposed to be the effects of bile. "I don't think I shall live long," he then said to a friend; "my mind will--must work itself out, and the body will soon follow it." A strange confession for a boy to make! But he gave his physical health no fair chance. His life was all brain work, study, and competition. When he took exercise it was in sudden bursts, which did him more harm than good. Long walks in the Highlands jaded and exhausted him; and he returned to his brain-work unrested and unrefreshed.

It was during one of his forced walks of some twenty-four miles, in the neighborhood of Stirling, that he injured one of his feet, and he returned home seriously ill. The result was an abscess, disease of the ankle-joint, and a long agony, which ended in the amputation of the right foot. But he never relaxed in his labors. He was now writing, lecturing and teaching chemistry. Rheumatism and acute inflammation of the eye next attacked him, and were treated by cupping, blistering, and colchicum. Unable himself to write, he went on preparing his lectures, which he dictated to his sister. Pain haunted him day and night, and sleep was only forced by morphia. While in this state of general prostration symptoms of pulmonary disease began to show themselves. Yet he continued to give the weekly lectures to which he stood committed to the Edinburgh School of Arts. Not one was shirked, though their delivery, before a large audience, was a most exhausting duty. "Well, there's another nail put into my coffin," was the remark made on throwing off his top-coat on returning home; and a sleepless night almost invariably followed.

At twenty-seven, Wilson was lecturing ten, eleven, or more hours weekly, usually with setons or open blister-wounds upon him--his "bosom friends," he used to call them. He felt the shadow of death upon him, and he worked as if his days were numbered. "Don't be surprised," he wrote to a friend, "if any morning at breakfast you hear that I am gone." But while he said so, he did not in the least degree indulge in the feeling of sickly sentimentality. He worked on as cheerfully and hopefully as if in the very fullness of strength. "To none," said he, "is life so sweet as to those who have lost all fear of dying."

Sometimes he was compelled to desist from his labors by sheer debility, occasioned by loss of blood from the lungs; but after a few weeks' rest and change of air, he would return to his work, saying, "The water is rising in the well again!" Though disease had fastened on his lungs, and was spreading there, and though suffering from a distressing cough, he went on lecturing as usual. To add to his troubles, when one day endeavoring to recover himself from a stumble occasioned by his lameness, he overstrained his arm, and broke the bone near the shoulder. But he recovered from his successive accidents and illnesses in the most extraordinary way. The reed bent, but did not break; the storm passed, and it stood erect as before.

There was no worry, nor fever, nor fret about him; but instead, cheerfulness, patience and unfailing perseverance. His mind, amidst all his sufferings, remained perfectly calm and serene. He went about his daily work with an apparently charmed life, as if he had the strength of many men in him. Yet all the while he knew he was dying, his chief anxiety being to conceal his state from those about him at home, to whom the knowledge of his actual condition would have been inexpressibly distressing. "I am cheerful among strangers," he said, "and try to live day by day as a dying man."

He went on teaching as before--lecturing to the Architectural Institutes and to the School of Arts. One day, after a lecture before the latter institute, he lay down to rest, and was shortly awakened by the rupture of a blood-vessel, which occasioned him the loss of a considerable quantity of blood. He did not experience the despair and agony that Keats did on a like occasion, though he equally knew that the messenger of death had come, and was waiting for him. He appeared at the family meals as usual, and next day he lectured twice, punctually fulfilling his engagements; but the exertion of speaking was followed by a second attack of hemorrhage. He now became seriously ill, and it was doubted whether he would survive the night. But he did survive; and during his convalescence he was appointed to an important public office--that of director of the Scottish Industrial Museum, which involved a great amount of labor, as well as lecturing, in his capacity of professor of technology, which he held in connection with the office.

From this time forward, his "dear museum," as he called it, absorbed all his surplus energies. While busily occupied in collecting models and specimens for the museum, he filled up his odds-and-ends of time in lecturing in Ragged Schools and Medical Missionary Societies. He gave himself no rest, either of mind or body; and "to die working" was the fate he envied. His mind would not give in, but his poor body was forced to yield, and a sever attack of hemorrhage--bleeding from both lungs and stomach--compelled him to relax in his labors. "For a month, or some forty days," he wrote--"a dreadful Lent--the wind has blown geographically from 'Araby the blest,' but thermometrically from Iceland the accursed. I have been made a prisoner of war, hit by an icicle in the lungs, and have shivered and burned alternately for a large portion of the last month, and spat blood till I grew pale with coughing. Now I am better, and to-morrow I give my concluding lecture (on technology), thankful that I have contrived, notwithstanding all my troubles, to early on without missing a lecture to the last day of the Faculty of Arts, to which I belong."

How long was it to last? He himself began to wonder, for he had long felt his life as if ebbing away. At length he became languid, weary, and unfit for work; even the writing of a letter cost him a painful effort, and he felt "as if to lie down and sleep were the only things worth doing." Yet shortly after, to help a Sunday school, he wrote his "Five Gateways of Knowledge," as a lecture, and afterward expanded it into a book. He also recovered strength sufficient to enable him to proceed with his lectures to the institutions to which he belonged, besides on various occasions undertaking to do other people's work. "I am looked upon as being as mad," he wrote to his brother, "because on a hasty notice, I took a defaulting lecturer's place at the Philosophical Institution, and discoursed on the polarization of light . . . But I like work: it is a family weakness."

Then followed chronic *malaise*--sleepless nights, days of pain, and more spitting of blood. "My only painless moments." he says, "were when lecturing." In this state of prostration and disease, the indefatigable man undertook to write the "Life of Edward Forbes;" and he did it, like every thing he undertook, with admirable ability. He proceeded with his lectures as usual. To an association of teachers he delivered a discourse on the educational value of industrial science. After he had spoken to his audience for an hour, he left them to say whether he should go on or not, and they cheered him on to another half-hour's address. "It is curious," he wrote, "the feeling of having an audience, like clay in your hands, to mould for a season as you please. It is a terribly responsible power . . . I do not mean for a moment to imply that I am indifferent to the good opinion of others--far otherwise; but to gain this is much less a concern with me than to deserve it. It was not so once. I had no wish for unmerited praise, but I was too ready to settle that I did merit it. Now, the word DUTY seems to me the biggest word in the world, and is uppermost in all my serious doings."

That was written only about four months before his death. A little later he wrote: "I spin my thread of life from week to week, rather than from year to year." Constant attacks of bleeding from the lungs sapped his little remaining strength, but did not altogether disable him from lecturing. He was amused by one of his friends proposing to put him under trustees for the purpose of looking after his health. But he would not be restrained from working so long as a vestige of strength remained.

One day, in the autumn of 1859, he returned from his customary lecture in the University of Edinburgh with a severe pain in his side. He was scarcely able to crawl up stairs. Medical aid was sent for, and he was pronounced to be suffering from pleurisy and inflammation of the lungs. His enfeebled frame was ill able to resist so severe a disease, and he sank peacefully to the rest he so longed for, after a few days' illness.

The life of George Wilson--so admirably and affectionately related by his sister--is probably one of the most marvelous records of pain and long-suffering, and yet of persistent, noble and useful work, that is to be found in the whole history of literature.

Instances of this heroic quality of self-forgetfulness in the interest of others are more frequent than we realize. Dr. Louis Albert Banks mentions the following illustration: "The other day, in one of our cities, two small boys signaled a street-car. When the car stopped it was noticed that one boy was lame. With much solicitude the other boy helped the cripple aboard, and, after telling the conductor to go ahead, returned to the sidewalk. The lame boy braced himself up in his seat so that he could look out of the car window, and the other passengers observed that at intervals the little fellow would wave his hand and smile. Following the direction of his glances, the passengers saw the other boy running along the sidewalk, straining every muscle to keep up with the car. They watched his pantomime in silence for a few blocks, and then a gentleman asked the lame boy who the other boy was: 'My brother,' was the prompt reply. 'Why does he not ride with you in the car?' was the next question. 'Because he hasn't any money,' answered the lame boy, sorrowfully. But the little runner--running that his crippled brother might ride-- had a face in which sorrow had no part, only the gladness of a self- denying soul. O my brother, you who long to do great service for the King and reach life's noblest triumph, here is your picture--willing to run that the crippled lives may ride, willing to bear one another's burdens, and so fulfill the law of Christ--that is the spirit of the King's country."

"The path of service is open to all, nay, we stumble on to the path daily without knowing it. Ivan Tourguenieff, in one of his beautiful poems in prose, says, 'I was walking in the street; a beggar stopped me--a frail old man. His inflamed, tearful eyes, blue lips, rough rags, disgusting sores--oh, how horribly poverty had disfigured the unhappy creature! He stretched out to me his red, swollen, filthy hands; he groaned and whimpered for alms. I felt in all my pockets; no purse, watch, or handkerchief did I find; I had left them all at home. The beggar waited, and his outstretched hand twitched and trembled. Embarrassed and confused, I seized his dirty hand and pressed it. 'Don't be vexed with me, brother; I have nothing with me, brother.' The beggar raised his bloodshot eyes to mine; his blue lips smiled, and he returned the pressure of my chilled fingers. 'Never mind, brother,' stammered he; 'thank you for this--this, too, was a gift, brother.' I felt that I, too, had received a gift from my brother. This is a line of service open to us all."

A gentleman writing to the Chicago *Interior*, relates this incident in his own career as a prosecuting attorney: a boy of fifteen was brought in for trial. He had no attorney, no witnesses and no friends. As the prosecuting attorney looked him over, he was pleased with his appearance. He had nothing of the hardened criminal about him. In fact, he was impressed that the prisoner was an unusually bright-looking little fellow. He found that the charge against him was burglary. There had been a fire in a dry goods store, where some of the merchandise had not been entirely consumed. The place had been boarded up to protect, for the time being, the damaged articles. Several boys, among them this defendant, had pulled off a board or two, and were helping themselves to the contents of the place, when the police arrived. The others got away, and this was the only one caught. The attorney asked the boy if he wanted a jury trial. He said "No;" that he was guilty, and preferred to plead guilty.

Upon the plea being entered, the prosecutor asked him where his home was. He replied that he had no home.

"Where are your parents?" was asked. He answered that they were both dead.

"Have you no relatives?" was the next question.

"Only a sister, who works out," was the answer.

"How long have you been in jail?"

"Two months."

"Has anyone been to see you during that time?"

"No, sir."

The last answer was very like a sob. The utterly forlorn and friendless condition of the boy, coupled with his frankness and pleasing presence, caused a lump to come into the lawyer's throat, and into the throats of many others, who were listening to the dialogue. Finally the attorney suggested to the judge that it was a pity to send the boy to the reformatory, and that what he needed more than anything else was a home.

By this time the court officials, jurors and spectators had crowded around, the better to hear what was being said. At this juncture one of the jurors addressed the court, and said: "Your honor, a year ago I lost my only boy. If he were alive, he would be about this boy's age. Ever since he died I have been wanting a boy. If you will let me have this little fellow, I'll give him a home, put him to work in my printing establishment, and treat him as if he were my own son."

The judge turned to the boy, and said: "This gentleman is a successful business man. Do you think, if you are given this splendid opportunity, you can make a man of yourself?"

"I'll try," very joyfully answered the boy.

"Very well; sign a recognizance, and go with the gentleman," said the judge.

A few minutes later the boy and his new friend left together, while tears of genuine pleasure stood in many eyes in the crowded courtroom. The lawyer, who signs his name to the story, declares that the boy turned out well, and proved to be worthy of his benefactor's kindness.

Deeds like that are waiting for the doing on every hand, and no man gives himself up to this spirit of helpfulness for others without strengthening his own life.

This spirit of self-forgetfulness and cheerful helpfulness is and essential quality of the true heroic soul--the soul that is not disturbed by circumstances, but goes on its way, strong and imparting strength.

We have to be on our guard against small troubles, which, by encouraging, we are apt to magnify into great ones. Indeed, the chief source of worry in the world is not real but imaginary evil--small vexations and trivial afflictions. In the presence of a great sorrow, all petty troubles disappear; but we are too ready to take some cherished misery to our bosom, and to pet it here. Very often it is the child of our fancy; and, forgetful of the many means of happiness which lie within our reach, we indulge this spoiled child of ours until it masters us. We shut the door against cheerfulness, and surround ourselves with gloom. The habit gives a coloring to our life. We grow querulous, moody and unsympathetic. Our conversation becomes full of regrets. We are harsh in our judgment of others. We are unsociable, and think everybody else is so. We make our breast a store-house of pain, which we inflict upon ourselves as well as upon others.

This disposition is encouraged by selfishness; indeed, it is, for the most part, selfishness unmingled, without any admixture of sympathy or consideration for the feelings of those about us. It is simply willfulness in the wrong direction. It is willful, because it might be avoided. Let the necessitarians argue as they may, freedom of will and action is the possession of every man and woman. It is sometimes our glory, and very often it is our shame; all depends upon the manner in which it is used. We can choose to look at the bright side of things or at the dark. We can follow good and eschew evil thoughts. We can be wrong-headed and wrong-hearted, or the reverse, as we ourselves determine. The world will be to each one of us very much what we make it. The cheerful are its real possessors, for the world belongs to those who enjoy it.

It must, however, be admitted that there are cases beyond the reach of the moralist. Once, when a miserable-looking dyspeptic called upon a leading physician, and laid his case before him, "Oh!" said the doctor, "you only want a good hearty laugh: go and see Grimaldi." "Alas!" said the miserable patient, "I am Grimaldi!" So, when Smollett, oppressed by disease, traveled over Europe in the hope of finding health, he saw everything through his own jaundiced eyes.

The restless, anxious, dissatisfied temper, that is ever ready to run and meet care half-way, is fatal to all happiness and peace of mind. How often do we see men and women set themselves about as if with stiff bristles, so that one dare scarcely approach them without fear of being pricked! For want of a little occasional command over one's temper, and amount of misery is occasioned in society which is positively frightful. Thus enjoyment is turned into bitterness, and life becomes like a journey barefooted among thorns and briers and prickles. "Though sometimes small evils," says Richard Sharp, "like invisible insects, inflict great pain, and a single hair may stop a vast machine, yet the chief secret of comfort lies in not suffering trifles to vex us; and in prudently cultivating and under-growth of small pleasures, since very few great ones, alas! are let on long leases."

Cheerfulness also accompanies patience, which is one of the main conditions of happiness and success in life. "He that will be served," says George Herbert, "must be patient." It was said of the cheerful and patient King Alfred that "good fortune accompanied him like a gift of God." Marlborough's expectant calmness was great, and a principal secret of his success as a general. "Patience will overcome all things," he wrote to Godolphin, in 1702. In the midst of a great emergency, while baffled and opposed by his allies, he said, "Having done all that is possible, we should submit with patience."

One of the chiefest of blessings is Hope, the most common of possessions; for, as Thales that philosopher said, "Even those who have nothing else have hope." Hope is the great helper of the poor. It has even been styled "the poor man's bread." It is also the sustainer and inspirer of great deeds. It is recorded of Alexander the Great that, when he succeeded to the throne of Macedon, he gave away among his friends the greater part of the estates which his father had left him; and when Perdiccas asked him what he reserved for himself, Alexander answered, "The greatest possession of all-- Hope!"

The pleasures of memory, however great, are stale compared with those of hope; for hope is the parent of all effort and endeavor; and "every gift of noble origin is breathed upon by Hope's perpetual breath." It may be said to be the moral engine that moves the world and keeps it in action; and at the end of all there stands before us what Robertson of Ellon styled "The Great Hope."

The qualities of the strong self-reliant man are sometimes accompanied by a brusqueness of manner that leas others to misjudge them. As Knox was retiring from the queen's presence on one occasion he overheard one of the royal attendants say to another, "He is not afraid!" Turning round upon them, he said: "And why should the pleasing face of a gentleman frighten me? I have looked on the faces of angry men, and yet have not been afraid beyond measure." When the Reformer, worn out by excess of labor and anxiety, was at length laid to his rest, the regent, looking down into the open grave, exclaimed in words which made a strong impression from their aptness and truth-- "There lies he who never feared the face of man!"

Luther also was thought by some to be a mere compound of violence and ruggedness. But, as in the case of Knox, the times in which he lived were rude and violent, and the work he had to do could scarcely have been accomplished with gentleness and suavity. To rouse Europe from its lethargy, he had to speak and write with force, and even vehemence. Yet Luther's vehemence was only in words. His apparently rude exterior covered a warm heart. In private life he was gentle, loving and affectionate. He was simple and homely, even to commonness. Fond of all common pleasures and enjoyments, he was any thing but an austere man or a bigot; for he was hearty, genial, and even "jolly." Luther was the common people's hero in his lifetime, and he remains so in Germany to this day.

Samuel Johnson was rude and often gruff in manner. But he had been brought up in a rough school. Poverty in early life had made him acquainted with strange companions. He had wandered in the streets with Savage for nights together, unable between them to raise money enough to pay for a bed. When his indomitable courage and industry at length secured for him a footing in society, he still bore upon him the scars of his early sorrow and struggles. He was by nature strong and robust, and his experience made him unaccommodating and self- asserting. When he was once asked why he was not invited to dine out as Garrick was, he answered, "Because great lords and ladies do not like to have their mouths stopped;" and Johnson was a notorious mouth-stopper, though what he said was always worth listening to.

Johnson's companions spoke of him as "Ursa Major;" but, as Goldsmith generously said of him, "No man alive has a more tender heart; he has nothing of the bear about him but his skin." The kindliness of Johnson's nature was shown on one occasion by the manner in which he assisted a supposed lady in crossing Fleet street. He gave her his arm and led her across, not observing that she was in liquor at the time. But the spirit of the act was not the less kind on that account. On the other hand, the conduct of the book-seller on whom Johnson once called to solicit employment, and who, regarding his athletic but uncouth person, told him he had better "go buy a porter's knot and carry trunks," in howsoever bland tones the advice might have been communicated, was simply brutal.

While captiousness of manner, and the habit of disputing and contradicting everything said, is chilling and repulsive, the opposite habit of assenting to, and sympathizing with, every statement made, or emotion expressed, is almost equally disagreeable. It is unmanly, and is felt to be dishonest. "It may seem difficult," says Richard Sharp, "to steer always between bluntness and plain- dealing, between giving merited praise and lavishing indiscriminate flattery; but it is very easy--good humor, kind heartedness and perfect simplicity, being all that are requisite to do what is right in the right way."

At the same time many are unpolite, not because they mean to be so, but because they are awkward, and perhaps know no better. Thus, when Gibbon had published the second and third volumes of his "Decline and Fall," the Duke of Cumberland met him one day, and accosted him with, "How do you do, Mr. Gibbon? I see you are always *at it* in the old way--*scribble, scribble, scribble*!" The duke probably intended to pay the author a compliment, but did not know how better to do it than in this blunt and apparently rude way.

Again, many persons are thought to be stiff, reserved and proud, when they are only shy. Shyness is characteristic of most people of Teutonic race. It has been styled "the English mania," but it pervades, to a greater or less degree, all the Northern nations. The average Frenchman or Irishman excels the average Englishman, German or American in courtesy and ease of manner, simply because it is his nature. They are more social and less self-dependent than men of Teutonic origin, more demonstrative and less reticent; they are more communicative, conversational, and freer in their intercourse with each other in all respects; while men of German race are comparatively stiff, reserved, shy and awkward. At the same time, a people may exhibit ease, gayety, and sprightliness of character, and yet possess no deeper qualities calculated to inspire respect. They may have every grace of manner, and yet be heartless, frivolous, selfish. The character may be on the surface only, and without any solid qualities for a foundation.

There can be no doubt as to which of the two sorts of people--the easy and graceful, or the stiff and awkward--it is most agreeable to meet either in business, in society, or in the casual intercourse of life. Which make the fastest friends, the truest men of their word, the most conscientious performers of their duty, is an entirely different matter.

As an epitome of good sound advice as to getting on in the world there has probably been nothing written so forcible, quaint and full of common sense a the following preface to an old Pennsylvanian Almanac, entitled "Poor Richard Improved," by the great philosopher, Benjamin Franklin. It is homely, simple, sensible and practical--a condensation of the proverbial wit, wisdom and every-day philosophy, useful at all times, and essentially so in the present day:

"COURTEOUS READER--I have heard that nothing gives an author so great pleasure as to find his works respectfully quoted by others. Judge, then, how much I must have been gratified by an incident I am going to relate to you. I stopped my horse lately where a great number of people were collected at an auction of merchants' goods. The hour of the sale not being come, they were conversing on the badness of the times, and one of the company called to a plain, clean old man with white locks, 'Pray, Father Abraham, what think you of the times? Will not these heavy taxes quite ruin the country? How shall we ever be able to pay them? What would you advise us to do?' Father Abraham stood up, and replied: 'If you would have my advice I will give it you in short, for, A word to the wise is enough, as poor Richard says.' They joined in desiring him to speak his mind, and gathering round him, he proceeded as follows:

"'Friends, the taxes are indeed very heavy, and if those laid on by the government were the only ones we had to pay we might more easily discharge them; but we have many others, and much more grievous to some of us. We are taxed twice as much by our idleness, three times as much by our pride, and four times as much by our folly; and from these taxes the commissioners cannot ease or deliver us, by allowing an abatement. However, let us hearken to good advice, and something may be done for us. God helps them that help themselves, as poor Richard says.

"'I. It would be thought a hard government that should tax its people one-tenth part of their time, to be employed in its service; but idleness taxes many of use more; sloth, by bringing on diseases, absolutely shortens life. Sloth, like rust, consumes faster than labor wears; while, The used key is always bright, as poor Richard says. But, Dost thou love life, then do not squander time, for that is the stuff life is made of, as poor Richard says. How much more than is necessary do we spend in sleep! forgetting that, The sleeping fox catches no poultry; and that, There will be sleeping in the grave, as poor Richard says.

"'If time be of all things the most precious, wasting time must be, as poor Richard says, the greatest prodigality; since, as he elsewhere tells us, Lost time is never found again; and, What we call time enough always proves little enough. Let us, then, be up and be doing, and doing to the purpose; so by diligence shall we do more, and with less perplexity. Sloth makes all things difficult, but industry all easy; and, He that riseth late must trot all day, and shall scarce overtake his business at night; while, Laziness travels so slowly that poverty soon overtakes him. Drive thy business, let not that drive thee; and Early to bed, and early to rise, makes a man healthy, wealthy and wise, as poor Richard says.

"'So what signifies wishing and hoping for better times? We may make these times better if we bestir ourselves. Industry need not risk, and, He that lives upon hopes will die fasting. There are no gains without pains; then, Help, hands, for I have no lands; or, if I have, they are smartly taxed. He that hath a trade, hath an estate; and, He that hath a calling, hath an office of profit and honor, as poor Richard says; but then the trade must be worked at, and the calling followed, or neither the estate nor the office will enable us to pay our taxes. If we are industrious we shall never starve; for, At the working man's house, hunger looks in, but dares not enter. Nor will the bailiff or the constable enter; for, Industry pays debts, while despair increaseth them. What though you have found no treasure, nor has any rich relation left you a legacy? Diligence is the mother of good luck, and God gives all things to industry. Then, plough deep, while sluggards sleep, and you shall have corn to sell and keep. Work while it is called to-day, for you know not how much you may be hindered to-morrow. One to-day is worth two to-morrows, as poor Richard says; and, farther, never leave that till to-morrow that you can do to-day. If you were a servant, would you not be shamed that a good master would catch you idle? Are you then your own master, be ashamed to catch yourself idle, when there is to be so much done for yourself, your family, your country, and your king. Handle your tools without mittens; remember that the cat in gloves catches no mice, as poor Richard says. It is true there is much to be done, and perhaps your are weak-handed; but stick to it steadily, and you will see great effects; for, Constant dropping wears away stones; and, By diligence and patience the mouse at in two the cable; and, Little strokes fell great oaks.

"'Methinks I hear some of you say, "Must a man afford himself no leisure?" I will tell thee, my friend, what poor Richard says--Employ thy time well if thou meanest to gain leisure; and since thou are not sure of a minute, throw not away an hour. Leisure is time for doing something useful. This leisure the diligent man will obtain, but the lazy man never; for a life of leisure and a life of laziness are two things. Many, without labor, would live by their wits only, but they break for want of stock; whereas industry gives comfort, and plenty, and respect. Fly pleasures, and they will follow you. The diligent spinner has a large shift; and, Now I have a sheep and a cow, everybody bids me goodmorrow.

"'II. But with our industry we must likewise be steady, settled and careful, and oversee our own affairs with our own eyes, and not trust to others; for, as poor Richard says--

"'I never saw an oft-removed tree, Nor yet an oft-removed family, That throve so well as those that settled be.

And again--Three removes as bad as a fire. And again--Keep thy shop, and thy shop will keep thee. And again--If you would have your business done, go; if not, send. And again--

"'He that by the plough would thrive Himself must either hold or drive.

And again--The eye of a master will do more work than both his hands. And again--Want of care does us more damage than want of knowledge. And again--Not to oversee workmen is to leave them your purse open. Trusting too much to others' care is the ruin of many; for, in the affairs of this world, men are saved, not by faith, but by the want of it. But a man's own care is profitable; for if you would have a faithful servant, and one that you like, serve yourself. A little neglect may cause great mischief; For want of a nail the shoe was lost; for want of a shoe the horse was lost; for want of a horse the rider was lost, being overtaken and slain by the enemy--all for want of a little care about a horse-shoe nail.

"'III. So much for industry, my friends, and attention to one's own business; but to these we must add frugality, if we would make our industry more certainly successful. A man may, if he knows not how to save as he gets, keep his nose to the grindstone all his life, and die not worth a groat at last. A fat kitchen makes a lean will; and

"'Many estates are spent in the getting, Since women for tea forsook spinning and knitting, And men for punch forsook hewing and splitting.

If you would be wealthy, think of saving as well as of getting. The Indies have not made Spain rich, because her outgoes are greater than her incomes.

"'Away, then, with your expensive follies, and you will not then have so much cause to complain of hard times, heavy taxes, and chargeable families; for

"'Women and wine, game and deceit, Make the wealth small and the want great.

"'And further--What maintains one vice would bring up two children. You may think, perhaps, that a little tea, or a little punch, now and then, diet a little more costly, clothes a little finer, and a little entertainment now and then, can be no great matter; but remember-- Many a little makes a nickel. Beware of little expenses--A small leak will sink a great ship, as poor Richard says. And moreover--Fools make feasts, and wise men eat them.

"' Here you are all got together at this sale of fineries and nick- nacks. You call them goods; but if you do not take care they will prove evils to some of you. You expect they will be sold cheap, and perhaps they may for less than they cost; but if you have no occasion for them they must be dear to you. Remember what poor Richard says-- Buy what thou hast no need of, and ere long thou shalt sell thy necessaries. And again--At a great pennyworth pause awhile. He means that the cheapness is apparent only, and not real; or the bargain, by straitening thee in thy business, may do thee more harm than good; for in another place he says--Many have been ruined by buying good pennyworths. Again--It is foolish to lay out money in a purchase of repentance; and yet this folly is practiced every day at auctions, for want of minding the almanac. Many a one, for the sake of finery on the back, has gone with a hungry belly and half-starved his family. Silks and satins, scarlet and velvets, put out the kitchen fire, as poor Richard says. These are not the necessaries of life; they can scarcely be called the conveniences; and yet, only because they look pretty, how many want to have them! By these, and other extravagances, the genteel are reduced to poverty, and forced to borrow of those whom they formerly despised, but who, through industry and frugality, have maintained their standing; in which case it appears plainly that, A ploughman on his legs is higher than a gentleman on his knees, as poor Richard says. Perhaps they have had a small estate left them, which they knew not the getting of; they think it is day and will never be night; that a little to be spent out of so much is not worth minding; but, Always taking out of the meal-tub, and never putting in, soon comes to be the bottom, as poor Richard says; and then, When the well is dry, they know the worth of water. But this they might have know before if they had taken his advice--If they would know the value of money, go and try to borrow some; for, He that goes a-borrowing goes a-sorrowing, as poor Richard says; and, indeed, so does he that lends to such people when he goes to get his own in again. Poor dick further advises, and says:

"'Fond pride or dress is sure a very curse,   Ere fancy you consult, consult your purse.

And again--Pride is as loud a beggar as want, and a great deal more saucy. When you have bought one fine thing, you must buy ten more, that your appearance may be all of a piece; but poor Dick says, It is easier to suppress the first desire, than to satisfy all that follow it. And it is as truly folly for the poor to ape the rich, as for the frog to swell in order to equal the ox.

"'Vessels large may venture more, But little boats should keep near shore.

It is, however, a folly soon punished; for, as poor Richard says, Pride that dines on vanity, sups on contempt. Pride breakfasted with plenty, dined with poverty, and supped with infamy. And, after all, of what use is this pride of appearance, for which so much is risked, so much is suffered? It cannot promote health, nor ease pain; it makes no increase of merit in the person; it creates envy; it hastens misfortune.

"'But what madness must it be to run in debt for these superfluities! We are offered, by the terms of this sale, six months credit; and that, perhaps, has induced some of us to attend it, because we cannot spare the ready money, and hope now to be fine without it. But, ah! think what you do when you run in debt; you give to another power over your liberty. If you cannot pay at the time, you will be ashamed to see your creditor; you will be in fear when you speak to him; you will make poor, pitiful, sneaking excuses, and, by degrees, come to lose your veracity, and sink into base, downright lying; for, The second vice is lying, the first is running in debt, as poor Richard says; and again, to the same purpose, Lying rides upon debt's back . .
.

"'And now, to conclude--Experience keeps a dear school, but fools will learn in no other, as poor Richard says, and scarce in that; for, it is true, We may give advice, but we cannot give conduct. However, remember this--They that will not be counseled, cannot be helped; and further, that, If you will not hear Reason, she will surely rap your knuckles, as poor Richard says.'

"Thus the old gentleman ended his harangue. The people heard it and approved the doctrine; and immediately practiced the contrary, just as if it had been a common sermon, for the auctioneer opened, and they began to buy extravagantly. I found the good man had thoroughly studied my almanacs, and digested all I had dropt on these topics during the course of twenty-five years."

The End.

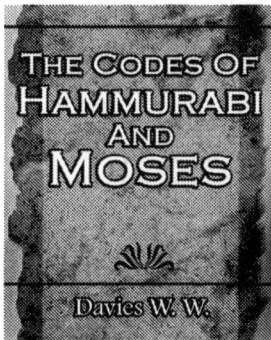

The Codes Of Hammurabi And Moses
W. W. Davies

QTY

The discovery of the Hammurabi Code is one of the greatest achievements of archaeology, and is of paramount interest, not only to the student of the Bible, but also to all those interested in ancient history...

Religion ISBN: *1-59462-338-4* **Pages:132**
MSRP $12.95

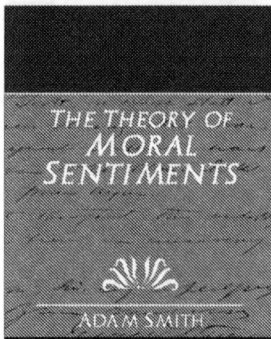

The Theory of Moral Sentiments
Adam Smith

QTY

This work from 1749. contains original theories of conscience amd moral judgment and it is the foundation for systemof morals.

Philosophy ISBN: *1-59462-777-0* **Pages:536**
MSRP $19.95

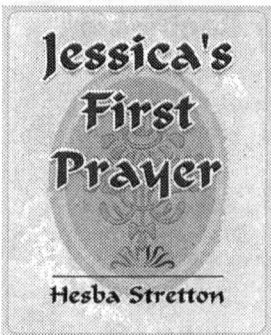

Jessica's First Prayer
Hesba Stretton

QTY

In a screened and secluded corner of one of the many railway-bridges which span the streets of London there could be seen a few years ago, from five o'clock every morning until half past eight, a tidily set-out coffee-stall, consisting of a trestle and board, upon which stood two large tin cans, with a small fire of charcoal burning under each so as to keep the coffee boiling during the early hours of the morning when the work-people were thronging into the city on their way to their daily toil...

Childrens ISBN: *1-59462-373-2* **Pages:84**
MSRP $9.95

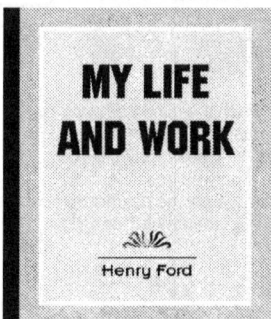

My Life and Work
Henry Ford

QTY

Henry Ford revolutionized the world with his implementation of mass production for the Model T automobile. Gain valuable business insight into his life and work with his own auto-biography... "We have only started on our development of our country we have not as yet, with all our talk of wonderful progress, done more than scratch the surface. The progress has been wonderful enough but..."

Biographies/ ISBN: *1-59462-198-5* **Pages:300**
MSRP $21.95

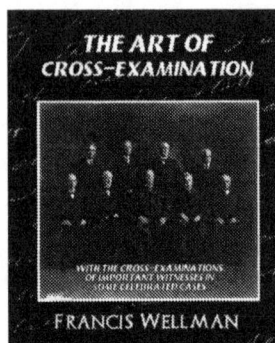

The Art of Cross-Examination
Francis Wellman

QTY

I presume it is the experience of every author, after his first book is published upon an important subject, to be almost overwhelmed with a wealth of ideas and illustrations which could readily have been included in his book, and which to his own mind, at least, seem to make a second edition inevitable. Such certainly was the case with me; and when the first edition had reached its sixth impression in five months, I rejoiced to learn that it seemed to my publishers that the book had met with a sufficiently favorable reception to justify a second and considerably enlarged edition. ..

Reference   ISBN: *1-59462-647-2*

Pages:412
MSRP $19.95

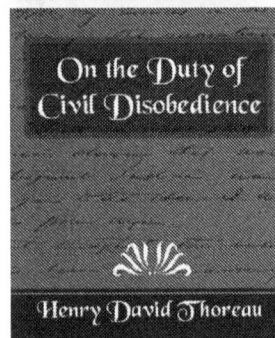

On the Duty of Civil Disobedience
Henry David Thoreau

QTY

Thoreau wrote his famous essay, On the Duty of Civil Disobedience, as a protest against an unjust but popular war and the immoral but popular institution of slave-owning. He did more than write—he declined to pay his taxes,   and was hauled off to gaol in consequence. Who can say how much this refusal of his hastened the end of the war and of slavery ?

Law   ISBN: *1-59462-747-9*

Pages:48
MSRP $7.45

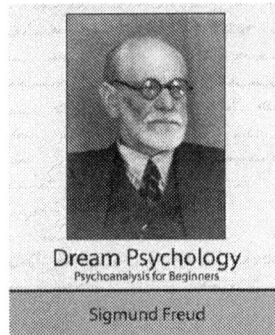

Dream Psychology Psychoanalysis for Beginners
Sigmund Freud

QTY

Sigmund Freud, born Sigismund Schlomo Freud (May 6, 1856 - September 23, 1939), was a Jewish-Austrian neurologist and psychiatrist who co-founded the psychoanalytic school of psychology. Freud is best known for his theories of the unconscious mind, especially involving the mechanism of repression; his redefinition of sexual desire as mobile and directed towards a wide variety of objects; and his therapeutic techniques, especially his understanding of transference in the therapeutic relationship and the presumed value of dreams as sources of insight into unconscious desires.

Psychology   ISBN: *1-59462-905-6*

Pages:196
MSRP $15.45

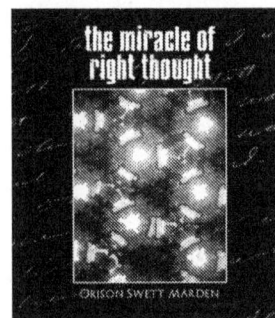

The Miracle of Right Thought
Orison Swett Marden

QTY

Believe with all of your heart that you will do what you were made to do. When the mind has once formed the habit of holding cheerful, happy, prosperous pictures, it will not be easy to form the opposite habit. It does not matter how improbable or how far away this realization may see, or how dark the prospects may be, if we visualize them as best we can, as vividly as possible, hold tenaciously to them and vigorously struggle to attain them, they will gradually become actualized, realized in the life. But a desire, a longing without endeavor, a yearning abandoned or held indifferently will vanish without realization.

Self Help   ISBN: *1-59462-644-8*

Pages:360
MSRP $25.45

The Rosicrucian Cosmo-Conception Mystic Christianity by *Max Heindel* ISBN: *1-59462-188-8* **$38.95**
The Rosicrucian Cosmo-conception is not dogmatic, neither does it appeal to any other authority than the reason of the student. It is; not controversial, but is: sent forth in the, hope that it may help to clear... New Age/Religion Pages 646

Abandonment To Divine Providence by *Jean-Pierre de Caussade* ISBN: *1-59462-228-0* **$25.95**
"The Rev. Jean Pierre de Caussade was one of the most remarkable spiritual writers of the Society of Jesus in France in the 18th Century. His death took place at Toulouse in 1751. His works have gone through many editions and have been republished... Inspirational/Religion Pages 400

Mental Chemistry by *Charles Haanel* ISBN: *1-59462-192-6* **$23.95**
Mental Chemistry allows the change of material conditions by combining and appropriately utilizing the power of the mind. Much like applied chemistry creates something new and unique out of careful combinations of chemicals the mastery of mental chemistry... New Age Pages 354

The Letters of Robert Browning and Elizabeth Barret Barrett 1845-1846 vol II ISBN: *1-59462-193-4* **$35.95**
by *Robert Browning and Elizabeth Barrett* Biographies Pages 596

Gleanings In Genesis (volume I) by *Arthur W. Pink* ISBN: *1-59462-130-6* **$27.45**
Appropriately has Genesis been termed "the seed plot of the Bible" for in it we have, in germ form, almost all of the great doctrines which are afterwards fully developed in the books of Scripture which follow... Religion/Inspirational Pages 420

The Master Key by *L. W. de Laurence* ISBN: *1-59462-001-6* **$30.95**
In no branch of human knowledge has there been a more lively increase of the spirit of research during the past few years than in the study of Psychology, Concentration and Mental Discipline. The requests for authentic lessons in Thought Control, Mental Discipline and... New Age/Business Pages 422

The Lesser Key Of Solomon Goetia by *L. W. de Laurence* ISBN: *1-59462-092-X* **$9.95**
This translation of the first book of the "Lemegton" which is now for the first time made accessible to students of Talismanic Magic was done, after careful collation and edition, from numerous Ancient Manuscripts in Hebrew, Latin, and French... New Age/Occult Pages 92

Rubaiyat Of Omar Khayyam by *Edward Fitzgerald* ISBN:*1-59462-332-5* **$13.95**
Edward Fitzgerald, whom the world has already learned, in spite of his own efforts to remain within the shadow of anonymity, to look upon as one of the rarest poets of the century, was born at Bredfield, in Suffolk, on the 31st of March, 1809. He was the third son of John Purcell... Music Pages 172

Ancient Law by *Henry Maine* ISBN: *1-59462-128-4* **$29.95**
The chief object of the following pages is to indicate some of the earliest ideas of mankind, as they are reflected in Ancient Law, and to point out the relation of those ideas to modern thought. Religion/History Pages 452

Far-Away Stories by *William J. Locke* ISBN: *1-59462-129-2* **$19.45**
"Good wine needs no bush, but a collection of mixed vintages does. And this book is just such a collection. Some of the stories I do not want to remain buried for ever in the museum files of dead magazine-numbers an author's not unpardonable vanity..." Fiction Pages 272

Life of David Crockett by *David Crockett* ISBN: *1-59462-250-7* **$27.45**
"Colonel David Crockett was one of the most remarkable men of the times in which he lived. Born in humble life, but gifted with a strong will, an indomitable courage, and unremitting perseverance... Biographies/New Age Pages 424

Lip-Reading by *Edward Nitchie* ISBN: *1-59462-206-X* **$25.95**
Edward B. Nitchie, founder of the New York School for the Hard of Hearing, now the Nitchie School of Lip-Reading, Inc, wrote "LIP-READING Principles and Practice". The development and perfecting of this meritorious work on lip-reading was an undertaking... How-to Pages 400

A Handbook of Suggestive Therapeutics, Applied Hypnotism, Psychic Science ISBN: *1-59462-214-0* **$24.95**
by *Henry Munro* Health/New Age/Health/Self-help Pages 376

A Doll's House: and Two Other Plays by *Henrik Ibsen* ISBN: *1-59462-112-8* **$19.95**
Henrik Ibsen created this classic when in revolutionary 1848 Rome. Introducing some striking concepts in playwriting for the realist genre, this play has been studied the world over. Fiction/Classics/Plays 308

The Light of Asia by *sir Edwin Arnold* ISBN: *1-59462-204-3* **$13.95**
In this poetic masterpiece, Edwin Arnold describes the life and teachings of Buddha. The man who was to become known as Buddha to the world was born as Prince Gautama of India but he rejected the worldly riches and abandoned the reigns of power when... Religion/History/Biographies Pages 170

The Complete Works of Guy de Maupassant by *Guy de Maupassant* ISBN: *1-59462-157-8* **$16.95**
"For days and days, nights and nights, I had dreamed of that first kiss which was to consecrate our engagement, and I knew not on what spot I should put my lips..." Fiction/Classics Pages 240

The Art of Cross-Examination by *Francis L. Wellman* ISBN: *1-59462-309-0* **$26.95**
Written by a renowned trial lawyer, Wellman imparts his experience and uses case studies to explain how to use psychology to extract desired information through questioning. How-to/Science/Reference Pages 408

Answered or Unanswered? by *Louisa Vaughan* ISBN: *1-59462-248-5* **$10.95**
Miracles of Faith in China Religion Pages 112

The Edinburgh Lectures on Mental Science (1909) by *Thomas* ISBN: *1-59462-008-3* **$11.95**
This book contains the substance of a course of lectures recently given by the writer in the Queen Street Hall, Edinburgh. Its purpose is to indicate the Natural Principles governing the relation between Mental Action and Material Conditions... New Age/Psychology Pages 148

Ayesha by *H. Rider Haggard* ISBN: *1-59462-301-5* **$24.95**
Verily and indeed it is the unexpected that happens! Probably if there was one person upon the earth from whom the Editor of this, and of a certain previous history, did not expect to hear again... Classics Pages 380

Ayala's Angel by *Anthony Trollope* ISBN: *1-59462-352-X* **$29.95**
The two girls were both pretty, but Lucy who was twenty-one who supposed to be simple and comparatively unattractive, whereas Ayala was credited, as her Bombwhat romantic name might show, with poetic charm and a taste for romance. Ayala when her father died was nineteen... Fiction Pages 484

The American Commonwealth by *James Bryce* ISBN: *1-59462-286-2* **$34.45**
An interpretation of American democratic political theory. It examines political mechanics and society from the perspective of Scotsman James Bryce Politics Pages 572

Stories of the Pilgrims by *Margaret P. Pumphrey* ISBN: *1-59462-116-0* **$17.95**
This book explores pilgrims religious oppression in England as well as their escape to Holland and eventual crossing to America on the Mayflower, and their early days in New England... History Pages 268

www.bookjungle.com *email: sales@bookjungle.com fax: 630-214-0564 mail: Book Jungle PO Box 2226 Champaign, IL 61825*

QTY

The Fasting Cure *by Sinclair Upton*   ISBN: *1-59462-222-1* **$13.95**
In the Cosmopolitan Magazine for May, 1910, and in the Contemporary Review (London) for April, 1910, I published an article dealing with my experiences in fasting. I have written a great many magazine articles, but never one which attracted so much attention... New Age/Self Help/Health Pages 164

Hebrew Astrology *by Sepharial*   ISBN: *1-59462-308-2* **$13.45**
In these days of advanced thinking it is a matter of common observation that we have left many of the old landmarks behind and that we are now pressing forward to greater heights and to a wider horizon than that which represented the mind-content of our progenitors... Astrology Pages 144

Thought Vibration or The Law of Attraction in the Thought World   ISBN: *1-59462-127-6* **$12.95**
by William Walker Atkinson   *Psychology/Religion Pages 144*

Optimism *by Helen Keller*   ISBN: *1-59462-108-X* **$15.95**
Helen Keller was blind, deaf, and mute since 19 months old, yet famously learned how to overcome these handicaps, communicate with the world, and spread her lectures promoting optimism. An inspiring read for everyone... Biographies/Inspirational Pages 84

Sara Crewe *by Frances Burnett*   ISBN: *1-59462-360-0* **$9.45**
In the first place, Miss Minchin lived in London. Her home was a large, dull, tall one, in a large, dull square, where all the houses were alike, and all the sparrows were alike, and where all the door-knockers made the same heavy sound... Childrens/Classic Pages 88

The Autobiography of Benjamin Franklin *by Benjamin Franklin*   ISBN: *1-59462-135-7* **$24.95**
The Autobiography of Benjamin Franklin has probably been more extensively read than any other American historical work, and no other book of its kind has had such ups and downs of fortune. Franklin lived for many years in England, where he was agent... Biographies/History Pages 332

Name	
Email	
Telephone	
Address	
City, State ZIP	-

☐ **Credit Card**   ☐ **Check / Money Order**

Credit Card Number	
Expiration Date	
Signature	

Please Mail to: Book Jungle
PO Box 2226
Champaign, IL 61825
or Fax to: 630-214-0564

ORDERING INFORMATION

web: *www.bookjungle.com*
email: *sales@bookjungle.com*
fax: *630-214-0564*
mail: *Book Jungle PO Box 2226 Champaign, IL 61825*
or PayPal *to sales@bookjungle.com*

Please contact us for bulk discounts

DIRECT-ORDER TERMS

20% Discount if You Order Two or More Books
Free Domestic Shipping!
Accepted: Master Card, Visa, Discover, American Express

www.ingramcontent.com/pod-product-compliance
Lightning Source LLC
Chambersburg PA
CBHW080701110426
42739CB00034B/3354